Rising Moon Ranch

Presents

The Art of Facilitation
with 28 Equine Assisted Activities

Charisse Rudolph & Brie

To see Charisse and Brie at work go to;
www.flickr.com/photos/healinghorses/
www.risingmoonranch.net   www.risingmoonranch.org

Editorial supervisor: Billie Jo Youmans. billiejoyoumans@gmail.com
Cover design: James at Humble Nations. Humblenations@gmail.com

The author of this book does not dispense medical advice or prescribe the use of any techniques as a form of treatment for physical, psychological, or medical problems without the advice of a physician, either directly or indirectly. The intent of the author is only to offer information of a general nature to help you in your quest for emotional well-being. Equine activities are highly active and participatory. Improper use of activities described herein may result in injury. In the event you use any of the information in this book for yourself, which is your constitutional right, the author and the publisher assume no responsibility for your actions.

Library of Congress Cataloging-in-Publication Data

Rudolph, Charisse.
    The Art of Facilitation, with 28 Equine Assisted Activities/ Charisse Rudolph

ISBN – 13 978-0692506172 ISBN – 10 0692506179
1. Animal-Therapeutic, 2. Horses, 3. Human animal relationships, 4 Processing/Facilitation 5. Equine Assisted Learning

First printing August 2015

The Healer and the Hunter

Not out for myself, searching for ways to succeed. All of me evaporates like water into air. Silently screaming, "Value me for my gifts are many." Walking a road under the surface, looking for openings to sprout.

Needing to be honored for who I am, my gifts from God. Tradition strangling my soul. Not recognized by many. Seen and honored by those who walk the same road. They say, "I recognize your soul." We are healers once separated to walk among the people.

How we long to reunite for understanding is what we seek. Healing is what we yearn, for earth's people and our own souls. Balance of traded energies to stay afloat. The battle of giving and receiving, nothing more than a good hunt, our biggest struggle.

Switching our minds to receive first, foreign to our thoughts. Wanting to thrive, we survive. Touching so many, raising their souls in our hands, giving a leg up, we lick our paws like a lion with a thorn.

Crying out, just guide me to succeed. Sitting in silence, waiting for an answer. Multi-talented, we add to our potential talents not being recognized, or valued by others, others who walk the surface of logic, tradition and fixed ideas.

We are the healers, the shamans of days gone by. Our struggles, staying true to our souls and being valued by those who only value what is common. Living in both worlds the world of the healer and the world of the hunter, we gasp for air, scratching the surface for our needs to be met.   © C.R.

DEDICATION

This book is dedicated to all of us who were pioneers in the field of experiential education. We each found our own niche as we branched off and added our unique passions to the work of serving others. You are forever my tribe.

Thank you to:

Randy Childs, for sharing your knowledge and passion of the outdoors, and for teaching me about experiential education.

Brad Childs, for hiring me to work for The Wilderness Institute (WI). You gave me my start.

Pam Nichols, for the deep, mindful conversations we have had throughout the years about life, facilitating, and serving.

Gail Martin-Mauser, for your courageous adventures facilitating all over the world. Your depth of passion and experience always shows me new possibilities.

Tina Johan, who gave me my very first taste of being a team builder/facilitator with Outward Bound, the urban program. Thank you for your guidance and friendship.

Margaret Colvin, although you have passed into a different dimension, I am so glad to have known and worked with you.

Kirk Clayton, who is a fellow naturalist, team builder, and always my friend.

Patrick Talbot, who is always sharing amazing ocean kayaking trips. Like many of us 'back in the day', you got your start at WI. I was so glad to find one of our tribe who became a Mental Health Specialist and could join my military programs. You are such a cool guy!

ACKNOWLEDGEMENT

I would like to acknowledge contributions from the Equine Growth and Learning Association (EAGALA) and its members. They have shared activities throughout the years and educated the world about equine-assisted learning and psychotherapy. Some of the equine-assisted activities in this book originated with EAGALA and their members even though the names and the implementation may have changed. www.eagala.org

I would like to thank the Professional Association of Therapeutic Horsemanship International (Path Int'l.) for being open to equine-assisted services as well as equine therapy. In 2014, Healing Horses & Armed Forces became a Premiere Accredited Center with PATH International. www.pathintl.org

I would also like to thank HeartMath® Institute, which I mention throughout the book. They have been most receptive and accommodating as I incorporated their techniques in my work with veterans, active military and their families. The HeartMath Institute techniques go beautifully with equine therapeutic services.

The HeartMath Institute provides feed-back instruments that connect to mobile phones or computers and allows individuals to monitor their own heart rate variability (HRV). The HeartMath Institute techniques are taught to assist individuals in balancing their heart, mind and nervous systems. Individuals dealing with anxiety, sleep disorders, overeating, addictions, or other life stressors need this assistance to think clearly and make better choices.

The equine link is that horses sense HRV instinctively. It is their natural instinct to be aware of danger so they can flee. Horses can add so much to our lives. They are calming and bring awareness. They mirror our energy and intention. Horses are not judgmental, so they are the perfect therapeutic partners. However, we cannot send horses home with everyone. Therefore, I became a coach, mentor, and licensed HeartMath trainer--and I thank them for their collaboration. www.HeartMath.org

I would like to thank Clifford E. Knapp, who was an Associate Professor of Curriculum and Instruction at Lorado Taft Field Campus at Northern Illinois University, when I first began my education in facilitation. Without the information he wrote that was shared with me in 1992, I would have not been able to understand the depth of facilitation. Clifford originally wrote many of the inserts you are about to read. I have reworked some of the copy but only to improve on word use and understanding.

I would also like to thank Kelly Arbaut who helped me on the book and serves as the mental health specialist in many of our programs. She has a non-profit, Kelly's Therapeutic Riders. Kelly is a ball of energy with whom I enjoy working very much. www.ktriders.org

INTRODUCTION

In therapy one looks back, in coaching one looks forward.

The purpose of this manual is to assist people who utilize the human-equine connection to improve the quality of life in the communities they serve.

Equine Assisted Activities (EAA) is a system that works with the horse's energy and intention. It does not include horsemanship. In EAA, the reaction of the horse reflects what is going on within a person's heart and mind.

This manual is a stepping-stone towards facilitating EAA. It is recommended that you acquire additional education in EAA before starting your own program.

I wrote this book because I realized I needed an activity manual. When a new client or group came to us, I would have to look through all my notes and come up with ideas to create a program plan. When we began to do one–on-one sessions with veterans, I realized our "bag of tricks" was limited. We needed to find 10-20 hours of activities that would meet the goals of our clients. The goals needed to be explained in order to meet PATH Intl. and Wounded Warriors scholarship program requirements.

In addition, I felt there was a need for more guidance in processing the experience. When facilitating EAA, it is important to elicit insight from your participants without interpreting their experience. This manual will provide questions that encourage participants to come up with their own answers. These questions have stood the test of time. I have used these questions since 1992, and they continue to be effective.

EAA is a process. Sometimes the answer will be obvious to you as the facilitator but not to the participant. Sometimes your participants or clients will see a piece of the puzzle; sometimes they will *get* a piece of the puzzle; and sometimes your clients will put the whole puzzle together. It all depends on where they are at in their emotional development. Just remember the old saying:

"You can lead a horse to water, but you can't make them drink."

Horses, team-building, kayaking, therapeutic art, cooking, drumming, or yoga can be added to any therapy to help others. In fact, any passion or hobby you have can be experiential in nature. Experiential education means that participants learn about themselves and others by participating in activities that bring meaning to their lives. By processing or discussing their thoughts, beliefs, behaviors, and patterns, they can change the way they react to stressful situations. Those who coach or facilitate ask questions that apply to the activity and the goal of the participant(s).

I was a member of the Association for Experiential Education for many years. The principles of experiential education are:

- Experiential learning occurs when carefully chosen experiences are supported by reflection, critical analysis, and synthesis.

- Experiences are structured to require the client to take initiative, make decisions, and be accountable for results.

- Throughout the experiential learning process, the client is actively engaged in posing questions, investigating, experimenting, being curious, solving problems, assuming responsibility, being creative and constructing meaning.

- Clients are engaged intellectually, emotionally, socially, soulfully, and/or physically. This involvement produces a perception that the learning task is authentic.

- The results of the learning are personal and form the basis for future experience and learning.

- Relationships are developed and nurtured: client to self, client to others, and client to the world at large.

- The client may experience success, failure, adventure, risk-taking, and uncertainty, because the outcomes of experience cannot totally be predicted.

- Opportunities are nurtured to explore and examine personal values.

- The facilitator's primary role includes setting suitable experiences, posing problems, setting boundaries, supporting clients, ensuring physical and emotional safety, and facilitating the learning process.

- The facilitator recognizes and encourages spontaneous opportunities for learning.

- Facilitators strive to be aware of their biases, judgments and preconceptions, as well as how these influence the client.

- The design of the learning experience includes the possibility of learning from natural consequences, mistakes, and successes.

This list from the www.aee.org website says it all. The beauty of bringing horses into the work is that they are living, breathing creatures that react to our energy, intention, and movement. Horses enhance the work of personal development with their beauty and grace. They give honest feedback, and because they live in the moment, they reflect back to us what we need to do to create change.

CONTENTS

OPENING POEM III

DEDICATION IV

ACKNOWLEDGEMENTS V

INTRODUCTION VI

PART 1
FORWARD TO THE ART OF FACILITATION 1

Chapter One   INTRODUCTION TO FACILITATING 7

Chapter Two   CATEGORIES' OF QUESTIONS FOR PROCESSING......................... 9

1. Communicating effectively   8. Asking for what you want

2. Expressing appropriate feelings   9. Making group decisions

3. Deferring judgment on others   10. Liking yourself

4. Listening   11. Cooperating

5. Appreciating self and others   12. Respecting commonalities

6. Leading others   13. Respecting differences

7. Following others   14. Trusting the group

Chapter Three   QUESTIONS TO ASK WHEN HORSES ARE INVOLVED.................... 15

Chapter Four   CLOSURE QUESTIONS 17

PART 2
FORWARD TO EQUINE ASSISTED SERVICES 18

Chapter Five UNDERSTANDING AND IMPLEMENTATION OF EAA 19

Chapter Six 22

1. ACTIVITY   IN THE PASTURE: 22

2. ACTIVITY   OBSERVE THE HERD: 24

3. ACTIVITY   INTUITION: 26

4. ACTIVITY   MOVING ENERGY: 28

5. ACTIVITY   TOUCH AWARENESS: 30

6. ACTIVITY   GROUND TIE: 32

7. ACTIVITY   OPEN MIND: 34

8. ACTIVITY   LIFE: 36

9. ACTIVITY   LEFT, RIGHT & CENTER: 38

10. ACTIVITY   STICK FIGURE: 40

11. ACTIVITY   COME TOGETHER: 42

12. ACTIVITY   JOIN UP: 44

13. ACTIVITY   NEW BEGINNINGS: 46

14. ACTIVITY   JOURNEY: 48

15. ACTIVITY   RESILIENCE: 50

16. ACTIVITY   TRADING PLACES: 52

17. ACTIVITY   GIVE AND TAKE: 54

18. ACTIVITY   COLORFUL COMMUNICATION: 56

19. ACTIVITY   CHAOS: 58

20. ACTIVITY   MAZE: 62

21. ACTIVITY   STORY TIME: 64

22. ACTIVITY   MOUNTAIN OR A GRAIN OF SAND: 66

23. ACTIVITY   BUCKET OF DREAMS: 68

24. ACTIVITY   MY WORLD: 70

25. ACTIVITY   DREAM CATCHER: 72

26. ACTIVITY   RUB, A DUB, DUB: 74

27. ACTIVITY   RED LIGHT, GREEN LIGHT: 76

28. ACTIVITY   WALK IN BALANCE: 78

29. ACTIVITY   BLIND WALK: ....(Surprise there are 29 activities.) 80

Chapter Seven   KEEPING TRACK OF PROGRESS AND INJURIES 82

Chapter Eight   EXAMPLE OF A PROGRAM PLAN 90

Bonus Chapter.. 97

LIVING THE DREAM 100

Rising Moon Ranch offers three *"Train the Trainer,"* Options.
   1. Grand Prix Information 102
   2. Sage Coaching Service Information 106
   3. One-Day, Boot Camp for Equine Assisted Coaching 110

Footnotes 112

PART 1
FORWARD TO

THE ART OF FACILITATION

Equine Assisted Activities (EAA) is closely related to Gestalt, which uses body language as a window to the soul. EAA techniques use body language (both horse and human) as the main communication tool. Energy and intention is the language that connects the human and the horse. In addition, as we facilitate, we must be aware of what we are projecting so we do not change the dynamics of the session. If a client is having a hard time dealing with trauma or a dilemma in his or her life, with the assistance of the horse and with an educated facilitator, time participating in EAA will be most effective.

The originator of Gestalt therapy, Dr. Fritz Perls, is quoted as saying, "The mission of therapy is not to explain things to the patient, but to provide them the opportunity to understand and discover him or herself." It is the same with coaching.

Facilitating is nothing more then being the eyes and ears for somebody else, asking questions from your observation of the activity, and inquiring about the client's choices while participating. When a person permits us to have a glimpse into their world, we are given the greatest gift: the gift of trust. All that is shared is held in our hearts and is confidential. We may see what looks like an obvious answer to our clients' conflict; however, what is right for us may not be the right answer for our clients.

In a sense, as facilitators or coaches, we hold their hands and take them to the pond so they can see their own reflection. Like the swan in the story of "The Ugly Duckling," who always wondered why she was not as good as everybody else, clients do not see themselves clearly. One day the 'duckling' saw her reflection and realized she was a beautiful swan. She had always been a beautiful swan but could not see her beauty or self-worth until she was ready. The same is true for our clients.

In this manual, activity and initiative, like processing and debriefing, are terms used interchangeably. The term facilitator refers to the individual who is leading the program or facilitating a group of participants during equine-assisted activities. For the purpose of being inclusive and sensitive to everyone and their title, when the term facilitator or equine coach is used, the person we are referring to may be a therapist, counselor, coach, equine specialist, mental health specialist, adventure educator or any other professional in the field of helping others.

DEFINING THE WORD PROCESSING

The primary role of Equine Assisted Coaching (EAC) is to assist clients in learning from their experience. Facilitators have the task of structuring experiences to encourage positive change in the learner or client. Change, according to **Schein** (1), is "the seeking out, processing, and utilization of information, attitudes, and behaviors."

EAC involves the processing aspect of the human experience and provides a format and strategy to assist coaches in learning and improving the skill of processing the experiences. The science of processing is also an art. This manual provides suggestions for facilitating both one-on-one and/or group processing sessions. The processing questions are organized under specific objectives. Additionally, there is a list of further readings on the topic is footnoted and sources printed at the end of this book.

People learn from experience. They can learn to use past experience to make future decisions, and therefore, change their behavior. According to **Norman Cousins** (2), "What is of the greatest consequence in a person's life is not just the nature and extent of his or her life but what has been learned from them."

Adventure educators use various structured activities in an outdoor setting to encourage the participants to understand themselves better. Usually activities such as backpacking, climbing, rappelling, kayaking, canoeing, camping, ropes courses, horses, and initiative challenges are planned to reach the goals of adventure-based programming. Typically, the skill of processing is applied after the activity to assist the participants in internalizing and generalizing the lessons learned. One underlying assumption in this article is that the skill of processing, or systematic questioning and analysis of an event, leads learners to greater self-awareness and assists them in applying what they gain in other life situations.

Adventure educators and other leaders in the helping professions need to develop specific techniques for processing the structured experiences of participants. Processing is a method for helping people reflect on recent experience and analyze the human interaction. It is a useful technique for examining personal growth and for building skills. The principle roles of a facilitator are observation and questioning, while at all times being focused on specific goals and objectives. Facilitating participants in problem-solving activities without the guidance of goals and objectives may result in haphazard learning or no learning at all.

PROGRAM GOALS AND OBJECTIVES

The goals, objectives, and benefits of the adventure-based counseling process has been described by **Walsh and Golins** (3) as follows,

"A set of characteristic problem-solving tasks set in a prescribed physical, social environment which impels the participant to mastery of these tasks and which in turn serves to recognize the meaning and direction of his or her life experience."

The primary reason facilitators must develop their own processing skills is to assist the participants in attaining program goals and objectives. In reviewing several research studies, there is little mention of the processing skills necessary for facilitators. Furthermore, little or no time is provided for this purpose in most scheduled trainings of initiative challenges such as equine-assisted activities, ropes courses, etc. Perhaps the goals and objectives of adventure programs would be better met by structuring more time for skilled facilitators to process experiences in specific areas of anticipated change. Other researchers support this contention.

According to **Rhodes** (4), "The primary purpose of an Outward Bound course is to provide the participant with an amount of experientially derived information about himself, his behaviors, attitudes, values, and his interaction with others which can be used, if he chooses, to bring about some personal changes in himself."

Silberman (5) challenged all educators and summarized these conclusions by stating, "The process of self-examination must be continuous. We must find ways of stimulating educators to think about what they are doing and why they are doing it."

THE EQUINE ASSISTED COACHES ROLE

The Equine Assisted Coach (EAC) facilitates initiatives or equine-assisted activities by asking questions. The EAC structures individual and group initiatives to meet specific related goals of the program. The function of the EAC is to create situations and learning climates in which participants encounter a challenge that can create stress. These initiatives often lead to success and the attainment of higher interpersonal skill levels. Sometimes success comes from not completing the equine-assisted activity. Completion of an activity is not success; a new understanding of the experience is the success of an activity.

Processing skills include the ability of the EAC to:

1. Observe the body language of the horse and human and make adequate inferences.
2. Listen to participants and create safety for emotions and self-disclosure.

3. Have an attitude of appreciation.
4. Allow group members to verbally state what went well during the initiative.
5. Defer judgment.
6. Allow participants to express thoughts and feelings.
7. Invite participants to express their needs and wants.
8. Question and inventory self. Allow the challenges to be about the participants.
9. Encourage the participants to acknowledge their personal limits.
10. Give useful feedback when requested.
11. Lead and follow.

An EAC models the following behaviors:

1. Accept the individual but not all behaviors.
2. Encourage self-disclosure.
3. Invite participants to explore self-examination.
4. Communicate effectively and ask questions.
5. Identify human relation issues. Tell them what you are noticing and ask for feedback.
6. Emphasize the "here and now" events. Be in the moment.

Before conducting problem-solving activities, the EAC needs to pay attention to certain ground rules and guidelines.

Lee Snooks (6) and others suggest the following:
1. Allow time for closure.
2. Direct conversation on a one-to-one basis.
3. Never allow the attacking of one's personal worth.
4. Foster acceptance of attitude toward the person's problem. *(It is real to them)*
5. Signify trust in individual for eventual solution.
6. Establishes the fact that individuals are unique and different.

Ann Beck, (7) in the Operations Manual for Hawaii Bound School, provides further guidelines for processing:

Self-Awareness: Keep in touch with your feelings. Where is your energy? Don't try to facilitate a processing session if you are distraught over some personal upset; resolve it first.

Attitude: The attitude that the leader exhibits sets the tone for the group. As a facilitator you should be alert, centered, show positive energy, keep your attention outward and remain flexible with the structure.

Acceptance: Allow everyone to be themselves. This requires listening, giving attention and being non-judgmental. It requires dealing with people in the present: where they are in their lives right now rather than where you would like them to be.

Focus: Be able to focus your attention and the group's attention on the person who is talking. Do not interrupt. Focusing lets the speaker know that he/she has your attention, your acceptance, and your aloha. *(Aloha is a Hawaiian word that means greeting or parting.)*

Drawing Out: Help others to clarify and articulate their feelings, thoughts, ideas, and values. Ask questions. It is often helpful to let a person hear back something they have said. This is referred to as reflective listening, or mirroring back what was stated.

Posture: Watch your posture and your body language. If you are slouched, closed, or outside, your "Ohana" will respond to that. *(Ohana means family. Family means nobody is left behind-or forgotten.)* "Clients and horses will respond to your energy whether it is open or shut down."

Physical Surroundings: Make sure that the physical surroundings are conducive to processing. Is it a place you will be comfortable in for an hour or more? A circle is generally the best formation for a group.

Energy Levels: Is everyone going to be able to stay awake? Can they put out the aloha that everyone needs?

Timing: Conduct processing debriefs immediately after each initiative. Do not wait for a few hours or days; much of the content and feelings will dissipate.

Weinstein, (8) outlines a "Trumpet Processing Guide" which lists a sequence of questions to guide problem solving. The guide can be a useful tool for processing group initiatives. The phases of the prescribed sequence are:

A. "What I hear you saying is..." (Confrontation and inventorying of responses.)
B. "What are you doing to solve the problem?" (Recognizing and clarifying function.)
C. "Is there something you keep doing that doesn't seem to solve your challenge?" (Owning pattern by clarifying function.)
D. "What are the costs of your behavior?" (Consequences)
E. "What are some other ways you could handle the situation?" (Alternatives)
F. "Is your method solving the problem?" (Evaluation)
G. "What choices do you have in solving this problem?" (Choice)

THE SCIENCE OF PROCESSING

The skills involved in processing an experience are complex. The science of processing has distinct limitations. The information shared up to this point has attempted to define, organize, and sequence specific components of the science of processing. Whenever possible, the knowledge of this science has been derived from careful and systematic observation of objects and events. It involves stating hypotheses and outcomes that depend upon logical thinking and experimenting. Processing skills involve the use of observations to expand our awareness of human behavior. However, there is also an art to processing an experience. Not everything can be reduced to an organized and sequential approach. *"This is especially true processing sessions with horses involved"*.

THE ART OF PROCESSING

The art of processing involves the creation of products; in this case, the product is an individual's knowledge about themselves and others in a group situation. The creation of these products involves the application of technical skills, knowledge, and feelings. The "artist," facilitator or EAC, must be flexible and respond with intuition and emotion at appropriate times as the situation warrants. It is difficult to instruct someone in the art of creating a safe learning climate, in asking the right questions, in accurately reading verbal and nonverbal human responses, and in sensing where participants are at in specific times during the initiative task. Some of these more advanced skills need to be learned over many years through awareness and internalized experience. There are certain human relation skills that, because of their complexity, take practice to master. There will always be room for art in processing the experience. (Advanced skills also include reading equine responses and sensing what the horse is communicating.)

The facilitator is the key to a safe and valuable learning experience for the participants in any experiential program. If those who facilitate practice the skills involved in successful processing with the same diligence that they practice riding horses, kayaking, camping, hiking, etc., the participants will be the benefactors of a broader and more useful education derived from direct experience.

Here are some suggested steps at the beginning of your event:

Convene with the group and begin the community building processing session.

1. Introduce yourself and explain how you view your role as a facilitator.
2. Initiate a "get-to-know each other" session with a structured group activity.
3. Allow participants to express some of their backgrounds, needs, expectations, and goals for the session.
4. Define the main purpose of the group and define all-important objectives that support this purpose.
5. Clarify the objectives by requisitioning feedback and input from the group.
6. Set and enforce selected limits, time constraints, space considerations, activity locations, group norms, and safety hazards.
7. Discuss how group decisions will be made. (i.e. consensus, majority vote, alternative leadership roles)
8. Throughout the session, decide when to intervene by directing a processing session, calling attention to group processes, norms, time factors; need for feedback, group roles, communication barriers, etc.

Children will ask questions not related to the activity. *This is how to address that challenge.* When asked a question that does not pertain to the activity, answer back with a question for them to think about. (Hidden Message)

If you have done the suggested steps above then you are ready to begin:

After explaining the initiative or the equine-assisted activity, ask the participants if they have any questions. Answer all questions and then ask the group if they would like a couple minutes to plan a strategy. If the participants decide not to plan a strategy but are not working cohesively, then ask them again how they would like to proceed. If they tell you they are 100% ready to begin the initiative, once they start, if they have more questions, suggest they get the answers from each other. In this way, they will begin to see the importance of planning, focusing, and working as a team.

When the team has completed the initiative, or feels they are complete with the task:

Ask everyone if they feel complete with the task or not. Some members of the group may not feel complete and may be ending their participation because the rest of their group seems to feel complete. This is when you ask the group members, **"What," "So What,"** and **"Now What."**

"WHAT?" - WHAT HAPPENED? "What" is the substance of the groups' interaction and what happened to the individuals? You look at the activity in relation to the objective(s) of the processing session. You can ask the participants, *"So, what happened?"*

"SO WHAT" - WHAT DID YOU GET FROM THE EXPERIENCE? "So what" is the difference the experience made to the individuals-the meaning for them. This term refers to transforming information and experience into relevant patterns of meaning. You can ask the participant, *"Did this experience change the way you could think about different situations in your life? "If the horse could talk, what would he tell you?"*

"NOW WHAT" - WHAT ACTIONS CAN YOU CHOOSE IN A SIMILAR SITUATION? "Now what," pertains to the decision about how to act on the experience by choosing the best alternative and reapplying them to other situations in the participants' lives. You can ask the participant, *"What can you do differently if a similar situation in your life occurs?" "What would be the best alternative you could use in similar situations?"*

You must realize that in designing a curriculum, in effective coaching, the way participants receive and process information will decide how the new information will be brought into their future. The questions **"What," "So What,"** and **"Now What,"** are important elements in allowing that to happen.

In addition, looking for metaphors during the activity can assist the participant to transfer what they experienced back to life. This is powerful because the participant carries with them a memory of something that they experienced. EAGALA points out that there is a potential metaphor in people, horses, equipment, physical placement, patterns, and feelings, as well as in the treatment team.

Chapter Two

Categories of Questions for Processing

1. Communicating effectively

A. Can anyone give an example of when you thought you communicated effectively with someone else in the group? (Consider verbal and nonverbal communications.)
B. How did you know that what you communicated was understood?
C. Who did not understand someone's effort to communicate?
D. What did not work in the communication attempt?
E. What could the communicator do differently next time to give a clearer message?
F. What could the message receiver do differently next time to understand the message?
G. How many different methods of communication were used?
H. Which ways were most effective? Why?
I. Did you learn something about communication that will be helpful later? If so, what?

2. Expressing appropriate feelings

A. Can anyone name a feeling they had at any point in completing the initiative? (Consider: angry, frustrated, hopeful, or enthusiastic.) Where in your body did you feel it most?
B. What was the thought behind the feeling?
C. Is there another time you remember having that feeling?
D. Did you express that feeling to others? If not, what did you do with the feeling?
E. Are your feelings more often expressed or suppressed?
F. Would you like to feel differently in a similar situation? If so, how would you like to feel?
G. What beliefs would you need to have in order to feel differently in a similar situation?
H. What would it take to believe what you are feeling?

I. How do you feel about conflict that may result from expressing certain feelings?
J. Did you notice how others responded during the initiative? Were their feelings being expressed?
K. What feeling is easiest to express? Which are more difficult?
L. Do you find it difficult to be aware of some feelings at times? If so, which ones?
M. Are some feelings not appropriate to express to the group at times? What feelings do you keep hidden?
N. What feelings were expressed non-verbally in the group?
O. Does expressing appropriate feelings help or hinder completing the initiative?

3. Differing judgment of others

A. Is it difficult for you to avoid judging others? Explain.
B. Can you think of examples of when you judged others in the group today?
C. Was there a judgment during the initiative?
D. What do you think were some of the advantages to your group by not judging them?
E. How does judging and not judging others affect the completion of the initiative?
F. Were some of the behaviors easier to dismiss than others?
G. In what situations would deferring judgment be helpful?
H. Can you think of any disadvantages of not judging others in the initiative?

4. Listening

A. Who made suggestions for completing the initiative?
B. Were all of these suggestions heard? Explain.
C. Which suggestions did you try?
D. What suggestions did the group ignore?
E. How did it feel to be heard when you made a suggestion?
F. What interfered with your ability to listen to others?
G. How could the groups' interference have been overcome?
H. Did you prevent yourself from listening? How?
I. Did you listen in the same way today as you generally do? If not, what was different about today?

5. Appreciating self and others

A. Who genuinely appreciated oneself and appreciated others in the group?
B. Did you express your appreciation to yourself and others? If so, how did you do this? (Verbal and nonverbal)

C. Would anyone want to share an appreciation now?
D. What expressions of appreciation were especially important for you to hear? Can you appreciate that in yourself as well?
E. What appreciations would you like to receive?
F. Do you usually ask for an appreciation/acknowledgement? Explain.
G. Do you usually give appreciations to yourself and others? Explain.
H. What did you do in the group that deserves appreciation?
I. What personal strengths, talents, gifts, or natural abilities do you have that you did not use today? Explain.

6. Leading others

A. Who assumed leadership roles during the initiative?
B. What were some of the behaviors you can describe that showed leadership?
C. Can everyone agree that these behaviors are traits of leaders?
D. How did the group respond to these leadership behaviors?
E. Who followed the leader even when you were not sure that the idea would work? Why?
F. Did the leadership role shift to other people during the initiative?
G. Who thought they were taking the leadership role? How did you do that?
H. Was it difficult to assume a leadership role with this group?
I. Why did some of you not take a leadership role?
J. Is it easier to take a leadership role in other situations or with different group members? Explain.
K. Did anyone try to lead the group but felt they were unsuccessful? What were some of the reasons for this? How did it feel to be disregarded?

7. Following others

A. Who assumed a follower role at times throughout the initiative? How did it feel?
B. How did you feel following different leaders?
C. Do you consider yourself a good follower? Was it an important role in the group today? Explain.
D. How does refusal to follow affect the leadership role?
E. What are the traits of a good follower?
F. How can you improve your ability to follow in the future?
G. Are followers as important as leaders? Explain.

8. Asking for what you want

A. Did you ask for all you wanted from the group members? Explain.
B. What prevented you from asking what you wanted?

C. What was the worst thing that could possibly have happened if you asked for what you wanted?

D. If everyone in the group asked for what they wanted how might it affect the completion of the initiative?

E. Do you need anything from the group members now? If so, what?

F. How do you feel when you ask for what you want and are refused or rejected? Did that happen today?

9. Making group decisions

A. How were group decisions made in completing the initiative?

B. Were you satisfied with the ways of making decisions? Explain.

C. Did the group arrive at any decisions through group consensus?

D. Did one or several individuals make the decisions?

E. Did everyone express his or her opinion when a choice was available? If not why?

F. What is the best way for this group to make decisions? Explain.

G. Do you respond in similar ways in other groups?

H. What did you like about how the group made decisions? What could you have done differently?

10. Liking yourself

A. Did anyone criticize or put him or herself down at any time?

B. What did you say to yourself?

C. At what point in the initiative did this happen?

D. Is this something you see in yourself in other situations? When?

E. Do you usually get upset with yourself and put yourself down when you make a mistake or don't feel perfect?

F. What sentence could you create to counteract the put-down message?

G. Were any others in the group aware that you were critical of yourself?

H. Do others in the group put themselves down in a similar way?

I. Is it possible that what you criticize in yourself could be considered a personal strength in other situations?

J. In what ways did you contribute to the initiative?

K. Which contribution made you feel the best about yourself?

L. Are you able to feel good about yourself even if you are not able to identify a contribution you made?

M. What are some abilities you have that you did not use in completing the initiative?

N. Why did you not use them?

11. Cooperating

A. Can you think of a specific example of when the group cooperated in completing the initiative? Explain.
B. How did it feel to cooperate?
C. Do you cooperate in most things you do?
D. How did you learn to cooperate?
E. What are the rewards of cooperation?
F. Are there any challenges associated with cooperation?
G. How did cooperative behavior lead to successfully completing the initiative?
H. How can you cooperate in other areas of your life?
I. Did you think anyone was blocking the group from cooperating? Explain.

12. Respecting commonalities

A. How are you like some of the others in the group?
B. Were these commonalities a help to the group or a hindrance in completing the task? Explain
C. Do you think you have other things in common with some of the group members that you have not found yet?
D. How did this initiative help you discover how you are similar?

13. Respecting differences

A. How are you different from some of the others in the group?
B. How do these differences strengthen the group as a whole?
C. When do these differences in people prevent reaching certain objectives?
D. What would this group be like if there were very few differences? How would you feel if this were so?
E. In what instances did being different help or hinder the group from reaching their objectives?
F. Do you usually view group differences as good, bad, or neither? Explain.
G. Did you become aware of any prejudices that you have towards people? If so, does that work for you?

14. Trusting the group

A. Can you give examples of when you trusted someone in the group? Explain.
B. Is it easier to trust some people and not others? Explain.
C. Can you think of examples when trusting someone could have been a poor idea?
D. How do you increase your level of trust for someone?
E. On a scale of 1-10, rate the level of trust you have in the group as a whole. Can you explain your rating?

F. What did you do today that deserves the trust of others?

G. How does the amount of fear you have affect your trust in others?

* Throughout the years working with teams I have used the above questions. The questions are still used when the horses are involved, however; we need to include questions that bring our equine partners wisdom into the activities. Remember, it is not our job as facilitators to make interpretations. It is our job to guide people to see things for themselves.

Chapter Three

Questions to Ask when Horses are Involved

Horses are living beings and part of the team. They are constantly looking to see who is in charge and if there are any discrepancies in the energy and intention that is being communicated. By reacting to our energy and intention, horses show us how we are res ponding to our challenges,if we can just learn to read them. Including horses in the process is so much richer than just using them for a team-building initiative or using a challenge course made up of poles and cables. Watch for the magic, make a few notes, and then ask the participants questions about the different activities. Below are some questions to consider.

1. What is happening with the horses?
2. What is working? What is not working?
3. What do you think the horses are doing, thinking, or feeling?
4. How does this relate to what you are doing, thinking or feeling?
5. What were the horses doing when _____?
6. What did you notice when the horses _____?
7. When the horses _____ I noticed you told us about____?
8. What did you think when the horses _____?
9. What did you say when the horses _____?
10. I noticed the horses _____. What do you think was going on?
11. When you tried _____ with the horse, what did you see, notice, think or feel?
12. What happened when you tried _____ with the horse?
13. How did the horse respond when you _____?
14. How did the other horses respond to_____; what happened when you reached the goal?
15. What was different or the same for each horse?
16. When the horses (or when you) entered the arena, what did you notice?
17. What was going on when_____?
18. Look at the horses. Why do you think they are reacting like that?
19. What could be going on for them?
20. What was happening when the horse lay down and rolled right next to you?

21. What did you decide that horses represented in this initiative?
22. The horses are all facing inside; what do you think is going on?
23. The horses have their ears back, nostrils flared, and they are lowering their heads and biting their teeth together. Why do you think they are they acting like that?
24. Are they showing signs of calmness, anger, frustration, or what?
25. Are your words, energy, and intention all working as one? What is the horse telling you?
26. What did the horses teach you today about yourself?
27. What did the horses teach you about other people?
28. What did the horse teach you about the importance of communication?
29. What did the horse teach you about working with a team?
30. What did the horse teach you about speaking up?
31. I noticed that as you were approaching the horses, they were backing up.
32. I noticed when you walked the horse over the bridge, you walked over it, and he stepped off the side.

Below is a possible series of questions that an Equine Specialist (ES) and Mental Health Specialist (MHS) might ask after an equine activity.

ES
What was the horse's reaction when you whispered your secret in his ear?
MHS
Is that a common reaction you get from _____?
MHS
What reaction would you like instead?
ES
Did you notice anything else about the other horses in the arena in reference to the secret and the horse you chose? Did you notice their body language?
ES
Why did you choose that particular horse?
MHS
If you could have your secret come true, what would that be like?

I suggest you always have a person on the team who understands the dynamics of processing the human experience and a person who specializes in understanding horses. Processing together is like a dance. Both of you need to learn how to work together, how to use your intuition on how many questions to ask, and what questions need asking. It all depends on the client, the day, the circumstance, and the sequence of the activity. All of this is in addition to the goal and what the participant wants to share.

In every program, there is a beginning, middle, and an end. The end is where you help your clients come to some conclusions, and they show appreciation for the day. At the end of the day, there is laughter and sometimes tears. This is your final contribution.

At our events, we usually share some form of take-home activity as well as the final questions. In addition, we recap some breathing techniques that we have used throughout the day. We also play music at different times-especially at the beginning and at the end of the event. You can create your event anyway you want. Be authentic, and it will shine through. Below are some closing questions to consider at the end of the day.

1. What did you learn about yourself?
2. What did you learn about others?
3. How did this day change your feelings about yourself and others?
4. What new questions do you have for yourself?
5. What did you do today that you are particularly proud of?
6. What skill are you working to improve?
7. Was your behavior today typical of the way you usually act in groups? Explain.
8. How can you use what you learned today in other life situations?
9. What beliefs about yourself and others were reinforced today?
10. Would you do anything differently if you were starting the initiatives again with this group?
11. What would you like to say to the group members?
12. What changes in your life would you like to make because of something you learned about yourself or others today?
13. What did you learn from the horses today?
14. What were the horses trying to communicate? If the horses were to whisper in your ear, what would they tell you as a parting word of encouragement?

PART 2

EQUINE ASSISTED SERVICES

There are several organizations that will give you certifications in equine-assisted services. Training and supervised practice is extremely important. There are many names associated with equine-assisted activities (EAA), but they all have one thing in common: "equine-assisted." You may hear people call it equine-assisted psychotherapy (EAP), equine-assisted learning (EAL), equine-assisted personal development (EAPD), or equine-assisted therapy (EAT). I like to use equine-assisted coaching (EAC) and equine-assisted services (EAS). Whatever you call it, it is an emerging field where horses and people collaborate to bring positive change and harmony to another person's life. However, EAS officially began in 1999 with the first recognized organization, the *Equine Assisted Growth and Learning Association* (EAGALA). In the EAGALA model, there is a collaborative effort between a licensed mental health specialist, an equine specialist, and a horse(s).

EAA are experiential in nature. This means that participants learn about themselves by participating in activities with the horse(s), and then they process or discuss behaviors and patterns that are discovered during the initiative. This approach has been compared to the ropes courses used by therapists, camps, coaches, treatment facilities, and human development courses around the world. EAS has the addition of utilizing the human-equine connection. This is a connection that is as old as the hills. Horses mirror our energy and intention; they look for our leadership.

Not all programs or individuals who collaborate with horses use this style of training. The focus of the modalities mentioned is not riding or horsemanship. It involves setting up initiatives involving horses, which will require the client or group to apply certain skills in order to be successful. Non-verbal communication, assertiveness, creative thinking, problem solving, taking responsibility, teamwork, relationships, confidence, and attitude are several examples. Being coherent is number one. Having your heart and brain work together cohesively is key. This approach has a powerful and incredible impact on individuals, youth, and families.

Chapter Five

Introduction to the Understanding and Implementation of EAA

Every client or group you work with will be different, and every time you do the same exercise, it will turn out different. Even if the group has the same participants, it will never turn out the same. The process and the conclusion will depend on the circumstances of the day. Where the participants are in their hearts and minds creates a unique experience every time.

The information found in this manual evolved from years of facilitating programs and recognizing the need for a book of one-on-one and group activities. Having activities at your fingertips increases your efficiency and effectiveness. As stated, some of these initiatives originated with EAGALA and/or EAGALA members. I also found ideas from YouTube videos; others I created from my team building days as the co-owner of Outdoor Learning Adventures. After the name of the activity, it states whether the activity is designed for one-on-one, group, or either. This makes it simple to find what you need to create your program or event. Being the CEO/Founder of the non-profit Healing Horses & Armed Forces, I needed to be able to get things done without wasting time.

I began my journey in EAS in 2001 with EAGALA and received "The Leadership Award for Contribution to Women" for EAS the following year. I received EAGALA Level 2 certification in 2011, and then began providing programs to military veterans and service-members suffering with Post Traumatic Stress (PTS). Two years later, I received my Equine Specialist in Mental Health certification with PATH Intl. The year following that, 2014, Rising Moon Ranch became a Premier Accredited Center with Path Intl. With so much going on in my life, I needed to create programs quickly, and that is the original reason I put this book together.

I am here to tell you that you can create whatever kind of program you want and work with whatever population you are passionate about serving. All the Healing Horses & Armed Forces programs begin with awareness exercises and an introduction to HeartMath®.

The HeartMath self-regulation techniques are scientifically proven to help people relieve stress and think more clearly. The simple explanation in their techniques help individuals get their emotions and brain to work in unison. We also offer drumming, therapeutic art, and yoga. The sky's the limit for what you can create at your events.

Charisse and Smokey listening intently.

Chapter Six
Activities

ACTIVITY 1

IN THE PASTURE (Either)

Objective:
- Awareness
- To be present

Activity:
Participants start in a circle, shoulder to shoulder, walking out 25 steps, being aware of their surroundings, noticing their feelings, and writing it down.

1. Tell the participant to get into a circle shoulder to shoulder facing out, walk 25 steps and write down what they observe using their five senses. We exclude the horses in this activity.
2. Ask them to write as many things as they can in _____minutes.
3. Then ask the participants to write down how what they observed made them feel. Here is an example; a participant might write down, "I hear the leaves rustling in the wind. When I hear that sound, I feel warm and loved, because it reminds me of fall, the nights getting cooler, and the wood burning stove warming the chill in the air." **Emotional awareness is important.** Not everyone can get to the feelings about what they may be sensing. Perhaps, it will only be a one-word description, which is fine.

Items needed:
- ❖ **Pencils**
- ❖ **Pocket Notebooks**

***Variations*:**
1. Sit or stand in a field, an arena, or open space, and have the client just begin to notice his or her surroundings using their five senses and write them down. Depending on your group, you could already have horses present. At our programs, we begin in a pasture or the field. We use this first equine activity as a way to ground people and bring them into the present. Then, we go to the arena and observe from the outside of the arena. The next thing participants do

after that is go into the arena and meet the herd. In addition, everyone receives a pen and a pocket notebook to remember insights throughout the day.

Observations:
    A. Are the participants writing things down?
    B. Is their body language changing?

"WHAT" HAPPENED? "SO WHAT" DID YOU GET FROM THE EXPERIENCE?
"NOW WHAT" ACTION CAN YOU CHOOSE IN A SIMILAR SITUATION?

Processing:
    A. What was it like to be in the moment?
    B. How often do you take time for yourself to notice your surroundings?
    C. Was this easy for you to do, or did you find it difficult? Why?
    D. What did you notice?
    E. Was one sense stronger than the other? Why do you think that is?
    F. What did you like about the exercise?
    G. What did you not like about the exercise?
    H. Would taking a few minutes each day to just be present benefit your life?
    I. If so, how do you want to add this into your life?

ACTIVITY 2

OBSERVE THE HERD (Either)

Objectives:
- Awareness
- Projections
- Understanding challenges

Activity:
1. Have several horses loose in the arena.
2. Have the participants make notes of what they are observing or ask them to say it out loud.
3. Ask the participants to write down what they are observing, or what the observation reminds them of in their own lives.

Items needed:
- ❖ **Pencils**
- ❖ **Pocket Notebooks:**

Variations:
1. Having props flung out everywhere in the arena makes it more interesting.

Observations:
A. Notice the expressions of the participants.
B. Note which part of the arena the participant goes to and if any horses take notice.
C. Notice what the horses are doing with the props and how they are relating to each other.
D. Notice if the participants are writing things down.
E. Observe the horse body language.

**"WHAT" HAPPENED? "SO WHAT" DID YOU GET FROM THE EXPERIENCE?
"NOW WHAT" ACTION CAN YOU CHOOSE IN A SIMILAR SITUATION?**

Processing:
A. What did you notice about the horses?
B. Did you see when _____ picked up the cone, and almost threw it at _____?
C. What was that all about?

D. I noticed that _____ was looking over the fence at you. What do you think the horse was thinking?
E. I saw some of you laughing, what was funny? Did it remind you of anything?
F. Did any of the horses react like anyone you know?

ACTIVITY 3

INTUITION (Either)

Objective:
- Awareness
- Confidence
- Enjoyment
- Introspection

Activity:
Ask the participants to go up to each horse silently and use their intuition about the character of each horse.

1. Pick out different parts of your own character in each horse.
2. Decide as a group or individual what each horse will represent for the day.
3. Clip what the horse will represent onto the horse's noseband or mane. You could also paint symbols on the horses that will be washed off at the end of the day as a type of ceremony.

Items needed:
- ❖ **Clips or Water-Soluble Paint**
- ❖ **Laminated Attributions**

Variations:
1. If the group is large, have them do the activity in pairs.
2. If you are working with couples, take turns with one participant being blindfolded. Allow the blindfolded participant to talk and say what they sense. (Being blindfolded depends on the community you are working with and what they have experienced in the past. Always ask permission.)
3. Instead of the noseband, let the group decide and tape what the horse represents on a bareback pad.
4. Change what the participants say to the horses. They can tell the horse a secret, or they can ask the horse to show them something about themselves they did not know. Be creative depending on what the participants need.

Observations:
A. How do the different participants approach the horses?
B. How do the horses respond to the different participants?

"WHAT" HAPPENED? "SO WHAT" DID YOU GET FROM THE EXPERIENCE? "NOW WHAT" ACTION CAN YOU CHOOSE IN A SIMILAR SITUATION?

Processing:

A. How did that experience go? What was that like?
B. Which horse do you think is most like you? Why?
C. Which horse seems more like your spouse? Why?
D. Did the horse seem to listen to you?
E. What was the horse's character like?
F. What would be a good name for him today?
G. Did you feel intimidated by the horse? What did you do to calm yourself?
H. What do you usually do to calm yourself?
I. Did this remind you of anything in particular?

* Again, the questions you ask are going to help the client see a path they can take to solve a challenge they are having or create something new in their lives. The questions I ask with clients who have experienced domestic violence, for instance, will be different than the questions of clients who are doing a leadership program.

ACTIVITY 4

MOVING ENERGY (Either)

Objective:
- Communication (listening and speaking)
- Cooperation
- Building rapport and trust

Activity:
Participants will figure out on their own how to halter a horse and walk it from point A to Point B as a pair, a team, or an individual. The halter doesn't have to be put on correctly.

1. Halter the horse that seems to be the most or the least like you. Or choose a horse that represents a part of you or the horse you are most attracted to. Another option is just halter the horse.

Items needed:
- ❖ **Horse(s)**   ❖ **Halters & Ropes**

Variations:
1. Do it in teams of two.
2. Do it in combo like Left, Right and Center (Activity 9).
3. Do it in a large group. Have them clasp hands or elbows. The person who is at the beginning and the end of the line can only use one of their hands. Their other hand must be connected to the person next to them. (Set up consequences if they break the rules.)

Observations:
A. Which horse do they choose and why?
B. How do they work as a team?
C. Do they ask for help?
D. Do they get frustrated because they want to do it the correct way?
E. Do they follow directions? If not, does anybody say anything?
F. What do you hear them say?
G. Watch the participants' and the horses' body language.
H. How is the horse reacting to their attempt?
> **"WHAT" HAPPENED? "SO WHAT" DID YOU GET FROM THE EXPERIENCE?**

"NOW WHAT" ACTION CAN YOU CHOOSE IN A SIMILAR SITUATION?

Processing:
A. Why did you choose that horse?
B. What did you like about the horse's character?
C. Who decided how the halter would go on?
D. Did either of you have another idea that you shared with your partner?
E. Did he or she hear your idea?
F. Are you both satisfied with the outcome?
G. What other ideas did you have?
H. Did you talk about a plan?

This is not about horsemanship. You do not tell them how to do the task. It is about the process of doing something unfamiliar and how they react and how the horse reacts.

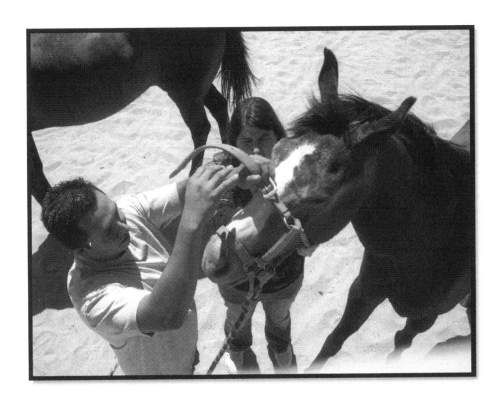

ACTIVITY 5

TOUCH AWARENESS / BRUSH/ PICK FEET (Either)

Objective:
- Awareness
- Compassion
- Overcoming apprehension
- Heart-Focused Breathing™

Activity:
1. Observe where the horse likes to be touched, where the touch is neutral and if there is a place that the horse is sore or does not want to be touched.
2. Brushing relaxes both the horse and participant; it helps conversation to flow. Our job is to bring attention to what the horse is communicating through the horse's body language. We do not make interpretations; we ask questions of the participant from the observations we make. For instance, picking up hooves is something a horse will do if you are coherent and in the right mindset. If not, you can try to pick up his foot, and it will not budge. If this was the case, we would ask our clients what they think is happening.

Items needed:
- **Brushes**
- **Hoof Pick**
- **Halter & Rope**
- **Horse(s)**

Variations:
1. Have participant identify four struggles they are dealing with and write them on 3x5 cards. Cards correspond to each leg of the horse; tape them on the cross ties, adjacent to each leg. Alternatively, you can use four cones to tape the cards onto (two in the front of the horse and two in the back).
2. Have participant breath in a renewed feeling to change the energy field around the struggles they have stated.

Observations:
A. Did the participant seem nervous?
B. Did the participant do the Quick Coherence® technique?
C. Did the participant pick up the horse's feet or decline?
D. Did the participant pick up all four feet?

E. Did they push through their fear?
F. How did the horse react to his front feet being picked up compared to his back feet?
G. What did you hear the participants say?

**"WHAT" HAPPENED? "SO WHAT" DID YOU GET FROM THE EXPERIENCE?
"NOW WHAT" ACTION CAN YOU CHOOSE IN A SIMILAR SITUATION?**

Processing:
A. How did you feel about doing this exercise?
B. What did you like and not like about it?
C. What was it like picking up the horse's feet?
D. Did you have the same feelings picking up the front feet as you did picking up the back feet?
E. If the client says the back feet were scary, you can ask: "How did you push past that fear?"
F. Is that what you have done in scary situations in your past?
G. What are some things you can do to get past that feeling?

I could go on forever on this one; it all depends on what the client reveals. Make sure the words they use (i.e. fear, sadness, or anxiety) are feelings they are labeling.

ACTIVITY 6

GROUND TIE (Either)

Objective
- To experience non-congruent communication.
- To feel empowered
- To choose the coping skills that are most beneficial.

Activity:
In this exercise the client or participant must ground tie the horse, which means the horse, must not move while the lead rope is on the ground.

1. Have the participant halter a horse, walk the horse down the arena and then ground tie him.
2. Have the participant walk around the horse and see if the horse will stay in place.
3. Each time the horse moves, the participant comes back to the horse's head and begins again.

Items needed:
- ❖ **Halter & Rope**
- ❖ **Horse(s)**

Variations:
1. Have two or more horses and participants. Do a team challenge that includes a time limit.
2. Have three participants connected by the hand or elbow, the one in the middle is the brain and can talk, the other two must listen and do what they are instructed to do. The outside two can only use the unattached hand.
3. Horse must keep its head up.
4. Instead of walking around the horse, brush the horse.
5. Circle the horse in different diameters.

Observations:
A. How does the client go about this exercise?
B. Does the client think the exercise was sufficient if the horse took a step during the challenge?
C. Does the client's body language, tone of voice, and words match?

D. Does the client use their voice?

E. How is the horse reacting?

"WHAT" HAPPENED? "SO WHAT" DID YOU GET FROM THE EXPERIENCE?
"NOW WHAT" ACTION CAN YOU CHOOSE IN A SIMILAR SITUATION?

Processing:

A. Where you successful?

B. When are you successful?

C. What makes success?

D. Did the horse understand your requests?

E. What do you do when people do not understand your requests?

F. How do you know when people understand your requests?

G. What can you do differently before you ask for a request?

H. Are you experiencing the same challenge with somebody in your life?

ACTIVITY 7

OPEN MIND: (One-on-one)

Objectives:
- To open one's mind and experience what it feels like to do something in a different way.
- To experience different levels of commitment.
- To allow participant to hear their internal process.

Activity:
1. Let the participant decide what each horse represents and what things they want to be opened-minded about. The horse can represent parts of the participant's character, intentions, possibilities, a relationship, a job, something their loved one is requesting, a new way of being, etc.
2. Fasten what the horse represents on the noseband of the horse's halters.
3. Have the participant build a three-sided enclosure in the arena. The enclosure can represent a person or a place.
4. Without the use of a lead rope or touching the halter, have the participant choose one of the three horses. Then, have the participant move the chosen horse into the enclosure. The horse **can** be touched but not bribed.
5. Have the participant say out loud everything they are thinking.

Items needed:
- ❖ Clips
- ❖ Paper & Felt Pen(s)
- ❖ Haltered Horse(s)
- ❖ Poles

Variations:
1. Use the round pen or big arena.
2. Have the participant choose only one horse in the arena.
3. Have some props in the arena sitting off to one side.

Observations:
A. What horse did the client choose for the activity?
B. Did the client get frustrated quickly?
C. Observe the body language of the client and horse.
D. Notice when the client's body language changes and what the horse does.
E. Notice the participant's level of commitment and when or if it changes.

F. Notice how the client touches the horse.

G. If other horses are in the arena, notice what they are doing.

"WHAT" HAPPENED? "SO WHAT" DID YOU GET FROM THE EXPERIENCE?
"NOW WHAT" ACTION CAN YOU CHOOSE IN A SIMILAR SITUATION?

Processing:

A. How was this exercise for you?

B. What feelings came up in the beginning, middle, and end?

C. Did you think you could do it?

D. Did you notice the other horses?

E. It looked as though one of the other horses was willing to participate. What was that all about?

F. Did you consider changing your choice of horses? Why?

G. Did you use all the options within your community?

H. Is this an example of what happens to you when you are feeling _____?

I. How would you like to be able to handle that?

J. What are some techniques that you use?

ACTIVITY 8

LIFE (Group)

Objectives:
- Learning to notice when emotions are being triggered.
- Connecting your energy to your intention.
- Nurtures teamwork, bonding and trust.
- Experience with "Heart Lock-In®" technique.

Activity:
1. Have the group stand in the center of the arena in a waiting zone, waiting to take their turn. Ask them to get coherent so they are able to think clearly and calmly. Ask them to think of something that will "lock-in" that coherent feeling so it can be used whenever needed.
2. On each of the four sides of the arena, have a three-sided enclosure set up. Let the four enclosures represent something important to the participant. For example: home, work, personal time, and responsibilities. Alternatively, the enclosures could represent achievements, pay raise, vacation, and success. Post what the participants have chosen on a clipboard; place a clipboard next to each of the four enclosures.
3. Have four horses loose in the arena and have each horse represent an attribute the participant would like to possess in order to gain what is important. Fasten the attribute onto the noseband of the halter.
4. Let each person have two minutes to get a horse into one of the enclosures, ground tie, and then walk around the horse.
5. The participant cannot touch or bribe the horse in anyway.
6. The horse can be haltered without the lead rope. However, the halter can only be touched if necessary, and only when the horse is in the chosen enclosure.

Items needed:
- Poles
- Barrels
- Four Clipboards
- Paper
- Felt Pens
- Clips
- Haltered Horses
- Laminated Attributes
- Horse(s

Variations:

1. Put a time limit on the exercise.
2. Allow the participant to touch the horse.
3. Have two teams.
4. Have a smaller arena.
5. Do in pairs.
6. Have each horse represent a challenge.

Observations:

A. Did the participants cheer for each other?
B. Did they share ideas?
C. What are some of the comments you heard?
D. If they were working in teams, did they help each other or sabotage each other?
E. Did they do what they were supposed to do all the way?
F. Was there consensus?
G. Who showed leadership?
H. Who was a good follower?
I. How did the horses react?
J. How did the horses and participants work together?
K. Did they show each other respect?

"WHAT" HAPPENED? "SO WHAT" DID YOU GET FROM THE EXPERIENCE? "NOW WHAT" ACTION CAN YOU CHOOSE IN A SIMILAR SITUATION?

Processing:

A. Who seemed to be leading this activity?
B. Was there anyone who thought the ideas were not going to work?
C. What did you do or say?
D. Was there anyone who wanted to give up?
E. What did it feel like when the horse got into the enclosure?
F. What do you regularly do when there are similar circumstances as this activity?
G. Did anyone take time with the horse to build a relationship?
H. Did you talk to one another?
I. Was there a plan or did everyone just do something different?

ACTIVITY 9

LEFT, RIGHT & CENTER (three)

Objectives:
- Allows the person in the center to gain confidence and learn to communicate clearly.
- Allows the person on the left and right side to support, build better listening skills, and gain trust in the center person's abilities.
- Nurtures teamwork, bonding, and trust.

Activity:
Three people will blanket and saddle a horse, working as a team.

1. This is an activity for three people.
2. The center participant is the thinker and communicator, and is in the middle of three people that are connected together at the elbows.
3. The other two people are on the left and right sides and must only do what the center person tells them to do. The person in the center will have them blanket and saddle the horse.
4. Only the person in the middle can speak and think.
5. The person on the right side is the right hand only; the person on the left side is the left hand only.
6. Again, all three participants are connected at the elbow.

Items needed:
- ❖ **Saddle Pad**
- ❖ **Saddle**
- ❖ **Horse(s)**

Variations:
1. Do it in two teams.
2. Allow it to be a timed event.

Observations:
A. Does the left and right side of the center participant stay quiet?
B. Do they struggle to work together?
C. Does the horse move around impatiently?
D. Does the center person find his or her voice?

"WHAT" HAPPENED? "SO WHAT" DID YOU GET FROM THE EXPERIENCE?
"NOW WHAT" ACTION CAN YOU CHOOSE IN A SIMILAR SITUATION?

Processing:

   A. How did it feel to be the participants on the left and right side--those who were listening and doing only what was told?

   B. How often did you do what you thought was needed without being told?

   C. Would any of you rather have had a different position? Why?

   D. How did it feel not being able to communicate?

   E. If the left and right side participants could say one word to the person in the center that was encouraging, what would it be?

   F. What did you do when you saw the horse getting fidgety?

   G. Did you try centering yourself with any techniques so you could think clearly and remain calm?

   H. If you did this exercise again, is there anything you would like to do different?

* Your observation and processing will depend on if this activity is done with a family, veterans, or work mates, etc. Remember: every activity is seed for your own ideas.

ACTIVITY 10

STICK FIGURE (One-on-one)

Objectives:
- To practice methods that calm anxiety.
- To see the importance of asking for help.
- To see that your challenges are possible to solve.
- To see that trying to control everything only adds stress to your life.

Activity:
This activity is for the client to realize that they need support in order to be successful.

1. Lay down a twenty to twenty-five foot stick human in the sand with poles in arena.
2. Put six buckets of feed, one each at the feet, arms, head and stomach of the stick figure. The stick figure represents the client.
3. The actual client represents his or her own will power or resilience.
4. The buckets of feed represent the vulnerable areas of the client's life.
5. In a large arena, five to six horses are introduced. Each horse represents a challenge in the client's life, such as spouse, work, bosses, food, alcohol, drugs, lack of sleep, or lack of fun.
6. The client is asked to keep the horses that represent the challenges they are facing away from the vulnerable areas.

Items needed:
- ❖ **Poles**
- ❖ **Six Buckets**
- ❖ **Feed**
- ❖ **Horses**
- ❖ **Paper & Felt Pens**
- ❖ **Tape**

Variations:
1. Have the client choose and name five vulnerable areas of the body then have the facilitators place the buckets of feed in those places.
2. Ask the client to come up with a consequence if the challenges (horses) eat any feed.
3. Use a different number of horses.
4. A different size of enclosure.

Observations:
   A. Does the client come up with creative ways to protect their vulnerable areas? Do they move the buckets to one spot? If so, change the rules and not allow the food to be moved. Or you can make that a rule from the start.
   B. Does the client keep the horses away at his or her own expense? Is the client getting exhausted or putting him/herself in danger trying to do the task alone?
   C. Does the client easily give into the horse's (challenges) or start out strong only to become less energetic?
   D. Does the client ask for some outside help?
   E. How did the client feel during the exercise?
   F. Did the client notice one particular horse (challenge) that was more difficult to keep away from the vulnerable areas? Did this correlate to the client's own experience?
   G. Could the client relate to what was happening in the way they tend to handle problems in their life?
   H. Was there a benefit in asking for help? Who could the helpers represent in the client's life (i.e. therapists, attorneys, doctors, a recovery group, sponsors, teachers, or college)?
   I. What type of consequence did the client choose?
   J. How did the consequence work out? Was it helpful or did it make things worse?

"WHAT" HAPPENED? "SO WHAT" DID YOU GET FROM THE EXPERIENCE?
"NOW WHAT" ACTION CAN YOU CHOOSE IN A SIMILAR SITUATION?

Processing:
   A. What were some of the ideas you had to protect the vulnerable areas of your life? (Buckets)
   B. What was it like trying to keep the horses away?
   C. Did you feel you could ask for help? Why or Why not?
   D. Was there one particular horse (challenge) more difficult than the others?
   E. Did it correlate with what is going on with your life?
   F. If this represents your life, what do you want to do different?
   G. When you were protecting one part of your life, what were the horses doing?
   H. How did your consequence relate to life?
   I. What is a consequence?

ACTIVITY 11

COME TOGETHER (Group)

Objectives:
- To work as a team.
- To rely on another and build trust.
- To learn how to think outside the box.
- To gain better communication, and listening skills.
- To make a habit of using Heart-Focused Breathing or Quick Coherence when triggered.

Activity:
The only rule in this activity is to move a horse over a jump in the arena, without bribing, or touching the horse. Set up a jump in the middle of the arena and place a pole on the ground right under the jump.

Items needed:
- ❖ **2 Tires, or Jump Standards**
- ❖ **2 Jump Poles**
- ❖ **Horse(s)**

Variations:
1. Have two teams create a jump no taller than 2'5" for the opposite team. Each team will have a horse and will create a jump for the other team.
2. Try giving different rules.
3. Have more than one horse.
4. Have a bucket of food across from the jump to be protected at all costs, and state what it could represent.
5. Let the participants use the props when they are creating the jump for the other team.
6. Use other items to hold up jump.

Observations:
A. Will they be kind and make an easy jump?
B. Will they help one another?
C. Have they utilized all their resources?
D. Are they competing?
E. Did the two groups cooperate or work together?

"WHAT" HAPPENED? "SO WHAT" DID YOU GET FROM THE EXPERIENCE?
"NOW WHAT" ACTION CAN YOU CHOOSE IN A SIMILAR SITUATION?

Processing:

A. How clear was your communication?
B. How was the horse reacting to what you were doing?
C. What was the horse communicating?
D. Who was the leader?
E. How did you decide on a plan to get the job done without being able to talk?
F. Did you always listen as you did in this activity?
G. If you had a similar situation at work or home, what are some things you could do differently?

ACTIVITY 12

JOIN UP (One-on-one)

Objectives:
- To recognize body language and mixed messages.
- To realize how others see you.
- To view how you react when triggered and how it affects others.
- To take responsibility for past intentions.
- To gain the understanding that body language and intent communicates more than our words.

Activity:

In this activity the client moves the horse around the round pen at different speeds and in different directions. This is an exercise that focuses on energy and how it affects others. It is a great example of how Heart-Focused Breathing and gaining coherency impacts situations. Also, I may ask the client to move the horse by first making a proclamation regarding their intention. For example, they might say out loud, "I am going to move this horse around with my energy and intention for the new job that I want."

1. To begin, you will have one horse and one person in the round pen at one time. With every fourth participant you will need to change horses.
2. The participant will have the horse move in different directions and at different gaits (walk, trot and canter), as well as asking the horse to stop. To do this, the participants will be using their energy and intent. All they may have in the round pen with them is a carrot stick without the lead line. If the client can become coherent while working the horse by the end of the activity, the horse will walk towards the client to join up. One of the goals is to stay in the center of the arena as much as possible.
3. In this activity, a person can learn about angry energy versus productive energy from the horse's movement. The participant will also be able to experience how they actually stop progress, when he or she is too far in front of their energy or too far behind their energy.

Items needed:
- ❖ **Horses to Take Turns**
- ❖ **Round Pen**
- ❖ **Carrot Stick Minus the Whip**

Variations:

1. Put a jump in the round ring along the rail.
2. Have the client say words that do not make sense. The horse responds to the words because of the energy of the word and intent. For instance, the word hamburger can be used out of context. I know this sounds silly; however, the client is able to hear their level of energy or commitment. (Note: There are two kinds of energy. *Anabolic energy* is constructive, expanding, fueling, healing, and growth orientated. *Catabolic energy* is draining. When using words with the horses that are *Catabolic*, the horses do not know who the herd leader is and the client will have a hard time getting the horse to move.)

Observations:

A. Is the client doing more running around than the horse?
B. Does the horse keep stopping?
C. Is the client's belly button and carrot stick pointing in front of the horse, behind the horse, or at the horse's hip?
D. What kind of energy is the client projecting with his or her voice?
E. Does the horse seem confused?
F. What is the horse's body language projecting?

"WHAT" HAPPENED? "SO WHAT" DID YOU GET FROM THE EXPERIENCE? "NOW WHAT" ACTION CAN YOU CHOOSE IN A SIMILAR SITUATION?

Processing:

A. How was that for you?
B. Did the horse meet your needs?
C. Can you relate that to other areas of your life?
D. *If the horse will not move, you might ask,* "Is there a place in your life that is not moving?"
E. I noticed you were behind the horse's energy a lot. What happens in life when you are behind other people's energy?
F. What happened to the horse when you were behind his energy?
G. How did you want the horse to react to your requests? How would that have looked?
H. What happens if you are way ahead of other people energy?
I. Do you ever feel that other people get in front of your energy? What happens?

I often process during this initiative. Throughout this book, I mention *Heart-Focused Breathing™ and the Quick Coherence® techniques* because I am a licensed HeartMath resilience trainer. Part of what I add to my programs is techniques that help people to think clearly and calm their nerves, stress or anxiety. *Because the horses read our energy and intention, these scientifically proven techniques complement each other beautifully.*

ACTIVITY 13

NEW BEGINNINGS (Either)

Objectives:
- To get clear and verbalize your goals.
- To focus on what you want.
- To intelligently plan for the future.
- To become aware of how you handle obstacles.

Activity:
In this activity participants will begin to look at his or her future needs and aspirations, and take a look at what obstacles they will need to overcome to achieve them.

1. Have three to four horses in the arena. Choose the horse you are attracted to the most.
2. Build a bridge to new beginnings. Choose obstacles that could get in your way of accomplishing that goal and put them inside the bridge.
3. Decide what you need to strengthen in yourself to get past those obstacles. Tape them onto the balls and carry them with you, or clip one word onto the horse's halter.

Items needed:
- Tape
- Paper or Index Cards
- Felt Pens
- Laminated Attributions
- Clips
- Haltered Horses
- Props
- Poles

Variations:
1. Tape them onto the horse's bareback pad.
2. Clip them in the horse's mane.
3. Have two teams and let each team build their own bridge and choose their own obstacles.

Observations:
A. How does the participant get the horse to the bridge?
B. Do the horses move willingly or put up a struggle?

C. Does the participant ask for assistance?

D. Do other members of the group offer assistance?

E. How does the participant approach the horse?

F. What obstacles did the participant choose?

"WHAT" HAPPENED? "SO WHAT" DID YOU GET FROM THE EXPERIENCE?
"NOW WHAT" ACTION CAN YOU CHOOSE IN A SIMILAR SITUATION?

Processing:

A. Why did you choose that horse?

B. What are your possible obstacles?

C. What did you do to get past the obstacles?

D. Did your horse cooperate?

E. Did you notice any body language of the horse that told you he didn't want to participate?

F. Was there any planning by the group to assist each other?

G. Did you focus on your breathing or heart rate while approaching the horse?

H. What conversation did you have going on in your head?

I. When obstacles seem to get in your way, what can you do to not let them win?

ACTIVITY 14

JOURNEY (Group)

Objectives:
- To develop team play and support.
- To increase communication.
- To build trust.

Activity:

As a team, the participants work together to get to safety, along with their equine friends.

1. Have four to twelve participants, and one to three horses. Go from Point (A) to Point (B), crossing an area you have created.
2. The only way to make it to the end is by stepping in the small hula-hoops.
3. No one can cross the finish line unless everybody on the team is past the starting line.
4. The hula-hoops must always be attended. If not, they will lose that hula-hoop or someone will be muted. Start out with one fewer hula-hoop than participants.
5. Find out what the horses represent and why it is necessary to have them on the journey.
6. Clip what the horse represents on the front of the noseband of the halter. Put the lead rope to one side. The horse can represent the necessities they will need while serving our country to stay coherent with Body, Mind, Heart, and Soul (i.e. food, first aid, determination, attitude, trust, support from home, God, faith, courage).
7. If a horse is let loose at anytime, the group loses what the horse represents, and they have to choose another need.

Items needed:
- **Small Hula-Hoops.**
- **Two Boundary Ropes**
- **Haltered Horses without Ropes**
- **Clips**
- **Attributes**

Variations:

1. Vary the number of hula-hoops (more, less or equal to the number of participants). Your variation should depend on the age of your participants, and the community.
2. Ask if there are any questions, and if they would like two minutes to plan.
3. Time the event.
4. Have a short twelve-inch rope connected to the horse's halter.
5. Vary the size of open space.
6. If not working with those being deployed, have the horses represent something else that pertains to your participants' needs.
7. Use 12 x 12 boards instead of small Hula-hoops.

Observations:
A. Are the participants coming together?
B. Does it look like there is a leader?
C. Are they following directions?
D. Are they handing off the horse or horses to each other?
E. What is there formation?
F. Are they in single file or supporting each other side by side?
G. How are the horses reacting?
H. Are the participants paying attention to how the horses are reacting?

**"WHAT" HAPPENED? "SO WHAT" DID YOU GET FROM THE EXPERIENCE?
"NOW WHAT" ACTION CAN YOU CHOOSE IN A SIMILAR SITUATION?**

Processing:
A. Did you work as a team? How was that?
B. Did you find that it was a difficult task?
C. How did you handle the task?
D. Was anyone in particular in charge?
E. How did the horses react?
F. Which ones seemed more willing? Why do you think that is?
G. What did you do about the horses that did not want to cooperate? What do you do when people in your life do not want to cooperate?

ACTIVITY 15

RESILIENCE (Group)

Objectives:
- To gain the realization that nonverbal communication is equally as loud as verbal communication.
- To explore your current beliefs and behaviors.
- To discover new behaviors for more effective living.
- To see that planning, clear communication, listening skills and working in a community are important to success.

Activity:
The objective is for the participant to realize how important it is to learn strategies to cope with his or her PTS.

1. Participants are asked to build two spaces utilizing various props in an arena setting. One space represents their time while being deployed; the second space represents civilian life at home.
2. The warriors are then asked to move a group of horses, without touching the horse, from the home space to the deployment space and back again. This is meant to represent their deployment transitions.
3. The warriors will determine what metaphor the horses represent. The horses may become a representation of themselves, family members, or feelings, expectations, strengths, dreams, or hopes.

Items needed:
- ❖ **Poles**
- ❖ **Props**
- ❖ **Horses**

Variations:
1. Instead of home and deployment, if you are working with other communities, change the spaces to represent, *Work and Home, Children and Spouse* or *Sobriety and Addiction.* Design what the spaces represent for your clients.

Observations:
1. Horses have different personalities, some may not want to get separated from the others, or one might not want to be brought to a certain area.

2. How do the participants go about this activity?
3. Which horses do they pick and how do they communicate with each other and the horses?
4. What do the participants build?
5. Did they take more time to build one area compared to the other?
6. How did the horses in the arena respond to the participants building each space? What meaning does that hold for the participants?
7. Did you see the participants body language change from one area to another?

"WHAT" HAPPENED? "SO WHAT" DID YOU GET FROM THE EXPERIENCE?
"NOW WHAT" ACTION CAN YOU CHOOSE IN A SIMILAR SITUATION?

Processing:
A. Can you tell us about the spaces you have created?
B. Why did you choose the horses that participated in this activity?
C. Who made the initial plan?
D. Did the plan change?
E. Were you working together the entire time?
F. Who had another idea that they thought would work better?
G. Did you tell your team about your idea? If not, what kept you from sharing your idea?
H. What were the horses doing that were not participating in the activity? What do you think they were thinking?
I. If you were to draw any parallels to life from this exercise, what would they be?
J. What do you think the horse is sensing about the different areas you have created? What were they doing while you were building your enclosures?

ACTIVITY 16

TRADING PLACES (Group)

Objectives
- To increase communication
- To build trust
- To gain comradeship and a support team

Activity
The goal is to get the horse(s) into each of the squares, for the count of five seconds. For it to count, the five seconds begins when the horse is standing still. This is a group activity.

1. Have four to twelve participants and two horses.
2. Set-up two starting lines for each group on different sides of the arena.
3. In between the starting lines, set up five or more squares that a horse can fit into. Have the squares evenly spaced apart.
4. Give each group a haltered horse without a lead rope.
5. This is a group exercise. There is forty-five seconds for each turn. When the time is up, one-team stops and the next team takes their turn.
6. Each group can decide to stop at any time before the forty-five seconds. Likewise, they can continue going and getting as many squares as they can in their forty-five second time-period.
7. There is no physical touching of the horse, halter, or the lead rope except when the horse is behind the starting line or in a square.
8. There is no bribing or simulated bribing.
9. No talking, except behind the starting line.
10. The horse may not go past the square that it needs to go into. (This is optional to make it harder.)
11. If the horse is in the square that the other team wants to put a horse into, the other team can push that horse out, and the team will have to go back to the previous square.
12. If a team breaks a rule, they need to start over.
13. If the horse does not remain stopped while waiting for the other team to finish their turn, they have to start over.
14. If stopped in a square, they can hold onto the horse's halter.

15. If they decide to risk getting to the next square and don't make it in time, they will have to keep the horse in the same spot but will not be able to touch him to keep him stopped.
16. Each team will choose a referee and timekeeper.

Items needed:
- **2 Haltered Horses**
- **A Time Watch**
- **A Timekeeper**
- **20 or more Poles (Garden Poles work well)**

Variations:
1. Allow the teams or different groups to communicate.
2. Set it up as two groups instead of teams.
3. Do not set a time limit on a turn, or if forty-five seconds is too short, change it.
4. Have them both start at the same time instead of taking turns.
5. If your group is small, have fewer squares in the middle (e.g. instead of five have three).
6. Allow a person to be blindfolded and while holding the horse be directed into a square.

Observations:
A. How long do they keep doing the same thing?
B. Do the groups help each other or compete and try to sabotage the other team?
C. How does the time factor affect their behaviors?
D. What happens when the horses are going to meet at a square? Does the group push the other one out, or do they work together?
E. When one group finishes, does the other group keep going or decide to finish, too?

"WHAT" HAPPENED? "SO WHAT" DID YOU GET FROM THE EXPERIENCE?
"NOW WHAT" ACTION CAN YOU CHOOSE IN A SIMILAR SITUATION?

Processing:
A. Who thought you were in competition? Why?
B. Who stressed out about the time? What could you have done differently?
C. What do you usually do to not feel stress?
D. How were the horses reacting? Did it mirror the way you were feeling?
E. What did the horse represent?
F. What part of this activity reminds you of your life?

ACTIVITY 17

GIVE AND TAKE (Pairs)

Objectives:
- Allow participants to recognize their own wants and needs.
- Allow the couple to be heard and assist in each other's desires.
- To give insight to each other's goals and fears.
- To establish clear communication.

Activity:
This is a great activity for couples. You can have one or several couples taking turns. We ask that the participants continue to go through the course until they feel satisfied and have met each other's needs.

1. Prior to participants or horses entering the arena, lay poles on the ground shaped in a narrow alley that expands to a large hexagon and then back to a narrow alley. Place a halter and two ropes in the middle of the hexagon. Stretch the ropes out to the left and right sides of the halter in the middle of the hexagon; make sure the hexagon is a foot wider than the halter and the two ropes. Remember to remove the halter and ropes before the participants arrive.

2. Have the participants pick out a goal they are working on as a couple or a goal they would like to add to the relationship. Have the couple write their goal on a 3X5 index card. Have participants choose a horse. Clip the goal onto the halter noseband or the mane of the horse. Examples of goals can include: more time together, finding a babysitter, or finding a better job.

3. Have them each choose some obstacles that could get in the way of reaching their combined or separate goal(s) from the props in the arena. Then, have them give a name to the obstacle and place it within the hexagon.

4. Place different lengths of lead ropes in a 5-gallon bucket. Have each participant reach into the bucket and take a lead rope. They have to use the first lead rope they pick up.

5. Each participant will hold a lead rope. The lead ropes will be attached to the right and left side of the horse's halter. The participants must walk on the outside of the alley/hexagon. The horses will walk on the inside only.

Items needed:
- ❖ **Poles**
- ❖ **Props**

- ❖ **Buckets of Feed or Horse Goodies**
- ❖ **3x5 index card**
- ❖ **Horses with Halters**
- ❖ **Different Lengths of Rope**
- ❖ **5 Gallon Bucket**
- ❖ **Clips**
- ❖ **Felt Pens**

Variations:

1. Have one-person walk the horse through the alley/hexagon being blindfolded. Have the other person verbally tell them what is needed in order to stay clear of the obstacles.
2. Create two teams. Put horse treats and extra obstacles into the alley to make it obviously unfair for only one of the teams. It will give you a lot to process!
3. For a child and their parents, have the child riding the horse, telling the parents what to do and how to be successful. The parents can only repeat what they hear and ask questions. (This variation is no longer EAGALA approved.)
4. When working with a couple, have each of them state aloud the other's goal and what they fear about reaching the goal out loud. The listener remains silent. Allow the couple to decide on an action they will take to reach the goal.

Observations:

A. Was one of the two pulled into the center alley? How did they handle that?
B. Did the horse keep on stopping in the middle? What did they do?
C. Did the horse dive into the goodies? What did they say the two buckets of grain or goodies represented?
D. Did they protect the different obstacles in the center? How?

"WHAT" HAPPENED? "SO WHAT" DID YOU GET FROM THE EXPERIENCE?
"NOW WHAT" ACTION CAN YOU CHOOSE IN A SIMILAR SITUATION?

Processing:

A. What happened?
B. What were the goals?
C. What are the possible obstacles?
D. Why did you choose that particular horse to work with, and who made the final decision?
E. What character did you appreciate in the horse you chose?
F. Did you think not having the same lengths of rope was fair?
G. What would be a good metaphor for this exercise?
H. After doing this activity, what changes in thinking would be beneficial to your goals?

ACTIVITY 18

COLORFUL COMMUNICATION (Two or more)

Objectives:
- To improve active listening
- To improve the ability to deliver a message and evaluate how the listener comprehends.
- To identify communication breakdowns as they occur.
- To practice communication behaviors in a non-threatening situation before entering real-life situations.
- To evaluate and determine strengths and weaknesses of communication patterns.
- To focus on strengthening verbal communication skills.
- To provide an opportunity to use new language skills: asking questions, clarifying, commenting, requesting, affirming, and denying.

Activity:
1. Have a horse standing, tied or held in a position, where it is safe for a person to be on both sides. Have one participant stand on the near side, and have one participant stand on the off side of the horse.
2. Give each person the exact set of materials for the activity.
3. Explain to the clients that the goal for today is to decorate the horse in such a manner that both sides look exactly the same. The horse can be decorated, or a story can be told using the paints.
4. One person is the designer. The role of the designer is to decorate the horse and then communicate to the other person what he or she has created. Then, that participant is to create the same thing on their side of the horse. They can only use words and cannot show the colors of the paint they are using.
5. The person on the other side of the horse can ask questions to clarify what the designer has told them.

Items Needed:
- ❖ **Non-Toxic Paints**
- ❖ **Paint Brushes**
- ❖ **Cross Ties or Hitching Rail**
- ❖ **Containers for Paint**
- ❖ **Haltered Horse**

Variations:

1. The designer cannot say the color but can give a hint. For example, "Use the color of the sky."
2. The communication must be sung.

Observations:

A. What is the general mood of the people participating?
B. How is the horse relating to the participants being on either side?
C. Is the communication improving as the activity goes on?
D. Are the participants actively listening?

"WHAT" HAPPENED? "SO WHAT" DID YOU GET FROM THE EXPERIENCE?
"NOW WHAT" ACTION CAN YOU CHOOSE IN A SIMILAR SITUATION?

Processing:

A. How did it feel to be listened to?
B. How did it feel being the listener?
C. Do both the listener and speaker have an equal amount of responsibility in communicating?
D. What made the process more clear?
E. What do you do differently when you are just talking to each other, without a horse in between you?
F. Did you notice a change in the horse's energy as the activity progressed? What do you think was happening?
G. Was this fun, aggravating, or what?
H. What would it take for the two of you to communicate like this all the time?
I. Before you began this activity were you and your partner in sync? What did you do?

ACTIVITY 19

CHAOS (Group)

Objectives:
- An understanding that giving up is not the answer.
- That everyone has challenges.
- That working as a team can be productive.
- To be able to connect and work together peacefully, accomplishing the goal by using the Heart-Focused Breathing or Quick Coherence techniques.

Activity:

This exercise is a group activity and is conducted in the arena with one horse, one halter, one lead rope, one bareback pad, and a bucket containing grooming supplies for the horse.

1. The items mentioned above are scattered about the arena.
2. Tell each participant their task separately, so others cannot hear what you have told them.
3. Participants are told they cannot reveal their task to anyone.
4. Participants must remain silent.
5. Have participants come up with consequences if they break the rules.
6. Encourage participants to use Heart-Focused Breathing or Quick Coherence techniques.

Task given can include:
1. Person one: halter a horse
2. Person two: brush a horse
3. Person three: put a bareback pad on the horse
4. Person four: lead the horse to a specific site in the arena
5. Person five: ground tie the horse

The ultimate goal is for the participants to work together.

Items Needed:
- 1 Horse
- 1 Halter
- 1 Lead Rope
- 1 Bareback Pad
- 1 Bucket Containing Grooming Supplies

Variations:

1. Write directions down on cards to be given to the participants ahead of time.
2. Make the activity a timed event.
3. Have the horse represent a specific issue and clip what was chosen on the horse's noseband.
4. If it is a large group do the exercise with several horses. Label the horses blue, green, red, and orange so it is clear who is working with what horse.
5. Label the horse's by what they represented earlier in the day.
6. Add braiding the horse's manes, picking up the horse's foot, taking notes, or drawing portraits of the horse.
7. Have some participants only focus on one horse, and other participant's focus on all the horses.
8. Participate in teams.

Observation:

A. Do participants hang back because there is too much going on?
B. Are some participants so driven to complete the goal that they do not consider others?
C. Who is trying to communicate? Are they being successful?
D. How are the horses reacting?
E. Do the individuals begin working on their tasks, or do they non-verbally attempt to work with the group?
F. Does the group remain focused, motivated, and energetic?
G. Do they get frustrated?
H. What happens in the group when the end is not known or discussed? Does everyone operate solely on the knowledge of his or her own task?
I. How did each participant respond and experience the activity? Were they frustrated, or overwhelmed?
J. What happened when an individual was unsure how to accomplish his or her task?
K. How did they respond to the horses and how did the horses respond to them?
L. How did the participants respond and interact with each other?
M. Did they notice anything that might help them perform, relate to, or understand their own situation?

"WHAT" HAPPENED? "SO WHAT" DID YOU GET FROM THE EXPERIENCE? "NOW WHAT" ACTION CAN YOU CHOOSE IN A SIMILAR SITUATION?

Processing:

A. What was that like?
B. How did you react to everything going on?
C. Were you able to get your job done?

D. Does this feel like real life? Why?
E. What were the horses doing?
F. If the horses could speak to you, what would they have told you?
G. How did you know when you were through?
H. What could you do differently if the same type of situation occurred?
I. What would be a good metaphor?
J. Did anyone try the Heart-Focused Breathing or Quick Coherence techniques?

Warning:
This is not meant to be a first activity. Cover any possible safety issues.

"You Don't Say?"

Activity 20

MAZE (Advanced Corporate Group)

Objectives:
- Team Work
- Focus
- Planning
- Leadership

Activity:
1. Set up nine squares in the arena using the poles prior to participants' arrival. Create a pattern or sequence that has to be followed from one side of the arena to the other. Write down the pattern of squares on a piece of paper, numbering them in a random sequence. Attach the paper to your clipboard, hidden from the participants.
2. Participants are to discover the pattern sequence by trial and error. Escorting the horse through the series of squares to the finish line.
3. The participants may not speak during this activity.
4. When the wrong square is chosen in the pattern a whistle will blow and the participant moves to the end of the line, losing their turn.
5. This activity may be done with two groups starting from opposite sides. The participants can have the same pattern or different patterns.
6. Label the horse's noseband with a goal that the participants want to achieve.

Items Needed:
- **Clipboard**
- **36 Poles or 36, 12" PVC Pipes**
- **Paper & Felt Pens**
- **Horse(s)**
- **Whistle**
- **A Pre-Determined Pattern**
- **Clips**
- **Haltered Horses with Ropes**

Variations:
1. You can do this with one group going in the same direction, or if you have enough staff that can assist you, the activity can be done with two groups going in the opposite directions.
2. You can set up as many spaces as you like.
3. You can use poles or ropes to make your squares.
4. Have the group members' help you observe what is going on.

5. Have more than one horse, each representing a different goal.

Observation:
    A. Do they work as a team?
    B. Does someone appoint him or herself to be the silent guide on the sidelines?
    C. If you have two groups, do they team up to work together, or do they compete?
    D. Do they take time to plan?
    E. Do people get really frustrated?

**"WHAT" HAPPENED? "SO WHAT" DID YOU GET FROM THE EXPERIENCE?
"NOW WHAT" ACTION CAN YOU CHOOSE IN A SIMILAR SITUATION?**

Processing:
    A. Did you understand the directions?
    B. How did staying silent affect you during this activity?
    C. What did the horse represent?
    D. What frustrated you the most?
    E. Were you worried about the other group getting the pattern before you did?
    F. Did you see them as the other team, or part of your team? Why?
    G. Does that seem like a familiar occurrence at work?
    H. Did the horse try to communicate with you at anytime during the activity?
    I. If you had to do it again, what would you do differently?

This can be a fun activity with a corporate program on a cool spring day. It would be a good activity after lunch or later in the day. I have done this activity many times with corporations. Participants really enjoy this activity, but it can also be frustrating and time consuming if done in the wrong sequence.

ACTIVITY 21

STORY TIME (One-on-one)
"Change the way you look at things and things you look at change" – Jack Canfield

Objective:
- To learn the simplicity in shifting negative thoughts to positive thoughts even when triggered.
- To learn how easy it is to change negative thoughts and attitudes to positive thoughts and attitudes when triggered by implementing the Heart-Focused Breathing technique on the go.

Activity:
In this activity the participant will observe the herd, and they will share two observations. Following breathing exercises and refocusing on positive experiences, their observations will change.

1. Have several horses loose in the arena with props scattered.
2. Using depleting emotions (i.e. frustration, depression, anger, hopelessness), ask the participant to give an identity to each of the horses.
3. Then, have the participant create a story about what he or she thinks is going on verbally, or have them write it down (e.g. "That horse is picking on the other one," or "That horse looks frustrated."). Tell them to be as descriptive as possible.
4. Next, have the participant do Quick Coherence, to get a renewing feeling such as enthusiasm, appreciation, courage, pride, happy, etc.
5. Then, have them observe the herd again and verbally express or write another story from that coherent, renewed feeling.
6. Compare the two stories.

Items Needed:
- **Paper & Pens**
- **Horses**
- **Props**

Variations:
1. Half-way through the exercise, have the participants paint or do a collage about their story. Then, do the renewed exercise as stated above, and do a second story and art interpretation. Compare the two stories and pieces of art.

2. Same as above but act out the stories in movement.
3. Storytelling in the herd can be used in an unlimited number of therapeutic situations and can address many issues. The horses always seem to offer a lot of story lines whether they are reactive or passive.
4. You can also introduce hay or other temptations into the arena to create new situations to observe and discuss. This is particularly appealing when working with a participant who is in a wheelchair or otherwise unable to spend an hour on their feet.

Observations:
A. How do the horses' reactions change?
B. What happens to the participant's body language?

**"WHAT" HAPPENED? "SO WHAT" DID YOU GET FROM THE EXPERIENCE?
"NOW WHAT" ACTION CAN YOU CHOOSE IN A SIMILAR SITUATION?**

Processing:
A. How do the two stories compare?
B. What made the stories different?
C. Did both stories feel real?
D. What is a story you tell that you could view differently?
E. What are some ways you can change a negative story or experience to a more positive outlook?

Through the years, I have found that when working with the horses, some people need more of a bridge to transfer the connection from the arena to life--especially, when it applies to trauma. That is why I show the participants methods while working with the horses to connect their heart, mind, and nervous system. The participants can then think clearly, and it allows them more of an opportunity to bridge their experiences.

ACTIVITY 22

MOUNTAIN OR A GRAIN OF SAND (One-on-one)

Objectives
- To name and realize fears and self doubts.
- To become aware, and find a method to go beyond and face the fear.
- To realize that everyone has attributes that can be of service if the attributes are recognized.

Activity:
1. Have three roped 10' diameter circles set up in the arena.
2. Have the participant name three or more challenges or goals they have in life, and help them put a name to that challenge. (Example: A participant shares that his/her workmate keeps bragging about how great they are, which annoys the participant. They may state that this makes them feel self-doubt, fear or anger.)
3. Have the participant decorate the spaces that represent those challenges or goals with the props that you have placed in the arena. (List of props are in the back of the book.)
4. Label the obstacles with 3x5 cards; tape them onto cones or the obstacle.
5. Next, have the participant choose an attribute to bypass the challenge. Ask them to tell you a time in their life they felt that attribute, and breath it in. *See back of book for a list of attributes.
6. Have the participant choose what horse they want to work with, and talk about what the horse could represent. (i.e. person in their life, a way they cope with pressure, a strength they can call on.)

Ask the participant to go through the different obstacles with the horses.

Items Needed:
- ❖ Ropes
- ❖ Props
- ❖ Horse
- ❖ 3x5 Index Cards
- ❖ Pens
- ❖ Tape
- ❖ Cones
- ❖ Attributes

Variations:
1. If there is more than one participant, one participant can lead the horse while the other participant is blindfolded.
2. If the participants are married, have one ride the horse facing

backwards or facing forward while the other one leads. (Riding the horse is not EAGALA Approved.)

3. Let the participant create the obstacles to match their challenges.

Observations

A. How much time does the participant take building the different areas?
B. How much drama goes into the story?
C. Does the participant want to explain things as they are building?
D. How attached are they to the story?
E. How many attributes do they choose?
F. Do they ask to use certain attributes for the different areas of their life?
G. How does the horse react to the different areas?

Once, I had a participant who had her three areas set up, and after she took the horse to the three different areas, we let the horse loose. The horse went and stood in the area that was her dream and inspiration. Could that have been where the energy felt the best?

**"WHAT" HAPPENED? "SO WHAT" DID YOU GET FROM THE EXPERIENCE?
"NOW WHAT" ACTION CAN YOU CHOOSE IN A SIMILAR SITUATION?**

Processing:

A. Can you pick an attribute each day and see how you can work that into your life?
B. What do you usually do when you come across a challenge? What could you do differently?
C. What are challenges and pre-imposed challenges? How do they differ?
D. Did you notice any similarities between the way the horse reacted to the obstacles and how you deal with obstacles in your life?
E. Did you learn anything? How might it help you to deal with challenges in your life?

ACTIVITY 23

BUCKET OF DREAMS (Group)

Objective:
- To work as a team
- To start thinking about goals and dreams
- To put importance and effort to your goals and dreams
- To set into motion the obtainment of your goals and dreams.

Activity:
1. Have a horse in the arena and set up two small jumps either twenty-four or thirty-six feet apart against the long side of the arena. Place a rope on the ground on the opposite side of the jumps, parallel to the arena fence. This encloses the area between the jumps. (If you stood in the center of the arena it would look like a jump on the left, a back fence, a jump on the right and a rope on the ground going from the right jump to the left jump.) The first jump is called the "Dream Idea," and the second jump is called the "Dream Attainment."
2. The horse needs to jump over the Dream Idea and then the Dream Attainment for the dreams to come true.
3. One person will start out with a bucket of burdens that has something to do with not obtaining dreams. Each person writes a burden on piece of paper, folds it up, tapes it to the rock and places it into the bucket. The bucket can never be put down. Each member on the team at some point must carry the bucket during the activity.
4. Another person will have a bucket of dreams. Each person will place a dream into the bucket. The dreams must never be put down. (Participants may label as confidential.)
5. Each time the horse jumps over both jumps, a person's dream is announced. Each time the horse <u>does not</u> jump over both jumps a person's burden is announced.
6. Let each person choose a dream from the bucket at the end and read it aloud (unless it is marked confidential).
7. Let people read aloud the possible burdens that could have stopped them from their dreams coming true.

Items Needed:
- ❖ **2 Buckets**
- ❖ **As Many Rocks as Participants**
- ❖ **2 Jumps**
- ❖ **6 Poles**

- ❖ **Paper & Pens**
- ❖ **Packing Tape**
- ❖ **Long Rope**
- ❖ **Horse**

Variations:

1. Have the horse jump over the two jumps as many times as there are people, or decide how many times the horse will jump over the two jumps for all dreams to come true.
2. Make the jumps higher or ask how high the participants want the jumps to be?
3. Put burdens on index cards and place them in the sand between the two jumps. Whenever the horse steps on a burden, read it to the group.
4. Have more than one horse in the arena.
5. Give them a time limit.

Observations:

1. How does the team work together?
2. Are there some who hold back?
3. Are there different ideas being shared?
4. What happened to the bucket of burdens?
5. What is the focus?
6. Are they more worried about their dreams, the bucket of burdens, or the task?

"WHAT" HAPPENED? "SO WHAT" DID YOU GET FROM THE EXPERIENCE?
"NOW WHAT" ACTION CAN YOU CHOOSE IN A SIMILAR SITUATION?

Processing:

1. Do you allow burdens to weigh you down?
2. How did it affect you knowing that at some point you had to take the burdens?
3. When was the horse most focused on your intent and energy?
4. What was your main focus? Was it the dreams, burdens, or the task?
5. Do you see any similarities in your life? Please explain.
6. What was the horse's role in this exercise? What did the horse represent?
7. Did you have any ah-ha moments?

ACTIVITY 24

MY WORLD (Either)

Objective:
- To realize how unmanageable life can be without the help of others.
- To recognize his or her needs for support in order to maintain healthy boundaries and relationships that will help him or her overcome their challenge.
- To practice overcoming stress in a safe environment.

Activity:
The participant is to keep the horses, which represent challenges the participant is trying to overcome away from the buckets of food, which represent important parts of the participant's life (i.e. relationships, activities, or goals). The participant stays within their circle of life, and directs the support team to meet his or her needs.

1. This activity was created for the round pen. Have the participant label six buckets of horse goodies and place them around the inside of the round pen walls. Each of the six buckets will be labeled with an important part of the participant's life (i.e. relationships, activities, goals, family, friends, education, career, hobbies, walking on the beach).
2. In the center, make a circle that represents the participant's life. Inside that circle of life, place some yummy hay.
3. Have one to three horses in the round pen that represent the diverse issues the participant is trying to overcome (i.e. fear, self-doubt, depression, anxiety, isolation, guilt, loneliness, perfectionism, control, shame, hopelessness, anger, PTS). Label what the participant chooses to work on and clip it onto the noseband of the horse's halter.
4. Have a support team of one to three facilitators available within the round pen. Then, ask the participant to label each member of the team(i.e. God, therapist, family, friends).
5. This is a good activity that can involve resilience techniques such as the Heart-Focused Breathing technique.
6. Participant is not to touch the horse(s).
7. Horse(s) are not allowed to eat.
8. Support team must stay linked together and may only move or help when directed by the participant.
9. Client must stay in the designated circle of life where the hay has been placed.

Items Needed:
- 6 Buckets
- Horse Goodies
- Hay
- Round Pen
- 1-3 Horses
- Halters
- Paper & Pens
- Clips
- Support Team

Variations:
1. Do not put hay in the center.
2. Have the client do the running around.
3. Build a stick figure and put the buckets at the two feet, two arms, and the head.
4. Use less buckets.

Observations:
A. Watch the participant's initial reaction to the challenge. Does he or she spend a lot of time trying to accomplish the goal alone?
B. Does the participant quit or give up easily?
C. Does the participant look frustrated? What does the participant do when they get frustrated or stressed by the activity?
D. Does the participant ask for help?
E. Does he or she remain focused, motivated, and energetic?
F. Does the participant use resources available to accomplish his or her goal?

"WHAT" HAPPENED? "SO WHAT" DID YOU GET FROM THE EXPERIENCE?
"NOW WHAT" ACTION CAN YOU CHOOSE IN A SIMILAR SITUATION?

Process: During and After
A. What did you experience? What did the support team experience?
B. What emotions did you feel during this activity? When did you feel the safest?
C. What did you find that was devouring or destroying your life? How was the horse demonstrating that?
D. What were some similarities between the horse's behavior and how your life is going?
E. How might this exercise benefit the understanding of you challenge?

* For closure the client may remove the labels from the feed buckets that represent those things that are important to the client's life.

ACTIVITY 25

DREAM CATCHER (Group)

Objective:
- To build bonds and realize we need to be able to depend on others to accomplish our goals.
- Build trust.
- Negotiate.
- To witness we all have struggles and dreams.
- To learn how becoming coherent can make a difference in any task.

Activity:
1. Divide group in half **(not teams)** and have two dream catchers, one at each end of the arena.
2. Use two barrels, cones, or jump standards for the dream catchers.
3. Ask each group to begin at opposite ends of the arena.
4. Have participants in each group agree on three to six goals or dreams they want to accomplish.
5. Have the groups write their dreams on full size pages of construction paper. Tell participants to write large so others can see what is written. Then, place the construction papers together on clipboards to be placed next to the dream catchers.
6. It is up to the group to get the horse through the different dream catchers in order for their dream to come to fruition.
7. When a group gets a dream, turn over a page on the clipboard, like a scoreboard, so the accomplished dream can be seen.
8. Have three horses loose in the arena and have participants choose which horse will be representing which dream.
9. No bribing the horse.
10. No touching the horse.
11. Participant may only use what is in their community (e.g. arena).

* Do not mention the word teams, as this will differentiate them by your words. If they come up with the idea that they can work together, great, let them. However, do not divulge that information. If they want to move the goal posts together, that is fine.

Items Needed:
- ❖ **Barrels or**
- ❖ **Cones or**
- ❖ **Jump Standards**
- ❖ **Construction Paper**
- ❖ **Felt Pens**
- ❖ **Clip Board(s)**
- ❖ **Clips**
- ❖ **Halters**
- ❖ **Horse(s)**

Variations:
1. Use less horses.
2. Use less goals or dreams.
3. Have only one dream catcher with fewer people and a smaller arena size.
4. If you are working with corporations you can call the Dream Catcher a Goal Catcher.

Observations:
A. How do they work together?
B. Do they help each other or compete?
C. Does anyone put himself or herself in harm's way?
D. What is going on with the different horses?
E. How do the participants separate the horses?

**"WHAT" HAPPENED? "SO WHAT" DID YOU GET FROM THE EXPERIENCE?
"NOW WHAT" ACTION CAN YOU CHOOSE IN A SIMILAR SITUATION?**

Processing:
A. Who thought there were two teams? Why?
B. Did you compete?
C. Did anyone communicate from the other group about their strategy?
D. Would it have been easier if you had known what the other strategy was?
E. How often when you are at home does the other person communicate the strategy of the day?
F. How about at work?
G. Who thought they had a great idea? Did you share it? How come?
H. Who showed appreciation for an idea or action? How did that make you feel?
I. What understanding can you take away about this activity?

* Remember that observations and processing will depend on the group you are contributing to. You need to know in which direction you want to guide the participants. Otherwise, if you are doing a corporate leadership program, you will not be observing or asking questions that have to do with intimacy. You must change the name and adjust some of the language of the initiative or activity.

ACTIVITY 26

RUB, A DUB, DUB (Group)

Objective:
- To become aware of outside distractions that can affect actions.
- To notice when anxiety or nerves are present that becoming coherent can change the situation.
- To see that focus is important in staying safe.

Activity:
Divide into small groups and wash horse(s). This requires the participants to be aware of their present surroundings, be in the moment, work together, be patient, and practice communication, which is necessary when dealing with trauma.

1. Participants must share water, supplies, and brushes.
2. Participants must work on the same side of the horse.
3. They must verbalize what they notice about the horse and their own inner voice.

Items Needed:
- ❖ Horse(s)
- ❖ Water
- ❖ Hose
- ❖ Bucket
- ❖ Shampoo
- ❖ Sponges
- ❖ Brushes

Variations:
1. Depending on the group and the wash rack area, let participants wash the horse on both sides at the same time.

Observations:
A. Are the participants working together?
B. Are they being respectful with each other?
C. Are they respecting the horse?
D. Are they showing signs of relaxation and enjoyment?
E. How is the horse reacting?

**"WHAT" HAPPENED? "SO WHAT" DID YOU GET FROM THE EXPERIENCE?
"NOW WHAT" ACTION CAN YOU CHOOSE IN A SIMILAR SITUATION?**

Processing:

A. What was the importance of communication in this activity? Discuss openness and the impact of verbalizing needs in completing the task.

B. What fears did the participants have?

C. What fears did the horse have?

D. How does fear affect your life?

E. What can you learn from the horse to help you with your own fears?

F. What can you do to work on your fears?

G. What happens if the participants or the horses avoid facing their fears?

H. How does a horse face its fear?

ACTIVITY 27

RED LIGHT, GREEN LIGHT (Group)

Objectives
1. To recognize need for support.
2. Recognizing how the projection of your energy can change how people see and treat you. To gain a better understanding of how your energy can change your boundaries and affect others.

Activity:
This activity shows how energy affects your life. The object of the game is to stop and start the miniature horses eating by playing the drums and working as a support team. The clients may move their chairs at will but may not remain standing.

1. Have participants label six buckets of horse goodies and set the buckets in the center of the round ring. Each bucket will be labeled as an important thing or event in the client's life (i.e. family friends, God, education, career, a goal or dream). This is a good time to ask participants to restate their goal from the beginning of the day.
2. The miniature horses will represent Post Traumatic Stress (PTS), Traumatic Brain Injury (TBI), or Military Sexual Trauma (MST). It is up to the participant to learn strategies to deal with the stress they have endured. They need to find ways to not allow their PTS (horses) to affect their lives, robbing them from the important quality relationships, activities, goals, or experiences they hope to have. They also need to be able to lighten their energy when they are triggered and upset.
3. In a drum circle, the participants will either allow or not allow the miniature horses to eat the goodies in the center.

Rules:
1. Allow the miniature horses to experience the goodies in the beginning by having them start out in the middle.
2. Each participant will have a place to sit and a drum. Make sure the chairs are separated enough so that the miniature horses can go in between the chairs. Leave enough space behind the chairs in the round pen as a get-away for the miniature horses.

3. Begin playing the drum softly so the miniature horses continue to enjoy the goodies.
4. Experiment with different levels of drumming and energy bringing the miniature horses to the middle a few times and to the outward edges of the round pen.
5. Avoid letting the horses slobber on the drums.
6. Have participants wash hands and remove rings before drumming.
7. There is no touching the horses.
8. Do not forget the HeartMath tools and techniques, because they really work with the horse's energy.

Items Needed:
- ❖ **Round Pen**
- ❖ **Horse(s)**
- ❖ **Drums**
- ❖ **Bucket**
- ❖ **Feed**

Variations:
1. Have one container of horse goodies.
2. Add singing or chanting.
3. Use other instruments.

Observations:
A. Is a lack of confidence in the participants breaking the flow of energy?
B. Are they focused and working together?
C. What is being said verbally and nonverbally?
D. How are the mini horses responding at different intervals?

"WHAT" HAPPENED? "SO WHAT" DID YOU GET FROM THE EXPERIENCE?
"NOW WHAT" ACTION CAN YOU CHOOSE IN A SIMILAR SITUATION?

Process: Do your processing during and after on this activity.
A. Ask the group what they felt or experienced.
B. Ask the group if they felt unsafe or overwhelmed?
C. Have the client point out similarities between the horses' behavior and his or her PTS.
D. Ask the client what he or she learned and how the insight will benefit them when triggered.

ACTIVITY 28

WALK IN BALANCE (One-on-one)

Objectives
1. To see if life is in balance.
2. To be able to prioritize what is most important.
3. To take a good look at what needs attention in your life.

Activity:
When a person gets out of balance, stress and upset occurs. Areas affected by imbalance are God, spirituality, family, health, friends, work, and play. These areas in life are all equally important. In this exercise, the participant gets to see how life is showing up for them and what part(s) need attention. The object of this activity is to allow the participant to set up and design up to six areas in the arena that represent different parts of the client's life.

1. This exercise is best in the big arena. Before the client enters, make sure you have all your props inside. At events, always say that the inside of the arena represents one's community.
2. Have the client choose which horse they want to collaborate with or just have the horse you choose already waiting inside the arena with your props. The props include buckets, stuffed animals, noodles, hula-hoops, poles, cones, etc.
3. Let the client tell you what he or she sees as the different parts of his or her life. Then have them tell you about the different areas that were chosen.
4. Let him or her explain why they chose the different props.

Items Needed:
- ❖ **Horse**
- ❖ **Props**
- ❖ **Poles**
- ❖ **Cones**

Variations:
1. Ask the client to identify three or four areas of their life that they would like to improve.
2. Lead the horse to each space and let him go within that space.

Observations:

    A. As the participant speaks, do they notice that one of the six areas mentioned above was not represented? If that happens, ask if they want to create something to represent that part.

    B. Notice, and ask the client, about the horse's energy and actions.

    C. Is the client projecting what is happening in the different parts of his or her life?

"WHAT" HAPPENED? "SO WHAT" DID YOU GET FROM THE EXPERIENCE?
"NOW WHAT" ACTION CAN YOU CHOOSE IN A SIMILAR SITUATION?

Process: During and After

    A. What is the horse doing?

    B. What do you think the horse is trying to tell you?

    E. Is there something in this part of your life that needs attention?

    F. How is this part of your life working for you?

    G. Is there something you would like to do different?

"Surprise!"
ACTIVITY 29

BLIND WALK (Partners)

Objectives
- To build trust with your partner or team.
- To enhance your verbal skills and listening skills.

Activity:
Blind walks are great for relationship work. Blind walks can be executed in a forest, at camp, in parks, at the ranch, and playfully with a partner at a mall. It is a trust and communication exercise; adding the horse enriches the activity. The horses can represent what ever the client thinks would be best.

1. Depending on your location and the general surroundings, have the person who is holding the horse blindfolded. Have the other person tell the blindfolded person what to do. The participants can hold hands, or hold a bandana or lead rope between them. They may start out unconnected, but soon, they will figure out they will be safer and more successful being connected.
2. Tell them the minimum amount of information.
3. You can set up an obstacle course in the arena, use a field, or walk around the ranch, maneuvering trees, rocks, or the natural landscape.

RULES:
1. The horse and the blindfolded person need to be cared for at all times and never left unattended.
2. Keep the rules brief. Ask if there are any questions.
3. Ask permission of the participant prior to using the blindfold. Depending on the person's life experiences, this may not be a good activity.
4. This is a silent activity. The person who is not blindfolded needs to watch for your signals and nonverbal direction.
5. Have participants take turns.
6. Ask the participants what the horse can represent in their life?

Items Needed:
- ❖ **Horse**
- ❖ **Bandana**
- ❖ **Halter & Rope**

Variations:

1. You can request the participants only speak in questions.
2. You can allow the blindfolded person to talk and have the person who can see only say yes or no.

"WHAT" HAPPENED? "SO WHAT" DID YOU GET FROM THE EXPERIENCE?
"NOW WHAT" ACTION CAN YOU CHOOSE IN A SIMILAR SITUATION?

Process:

A. What was it like being responsible for the horse and not being able to see?
B. Is this like something that is occurring in your life?
C. What was it like being responsible for your partner and the horse?
D. Did the horse end up representing what you thought he or she would represent, or did it change?
E. What was it like not being able to see, and being asked to trust your partner's judgment? * List of facilitating questions on judgment in chapter two.
F. Did you notice what the horse was doing when _____?
G. What do you think the horse was thinking when _____?
H. Do you think the horse felt safe when _____?

Choose questions based on what happened during the activity, but do not forget to ask about the horse's experience.

Chapter Seven.

Keeping Track of Progress and Injuries

When the clients have completed the program, it is time to debrief. You will discuss with your staff and volunteers the observations of the day. Keeping track of client progress is of utmost importance. Keeping track of what happened with the horses is equally important. With effective debriefing, you will begin to notice patterns in the horses and with the participants. When participants return, your observations from the previous program will be critical in preparing for your program outline.

Record the following information:

- Date?
- Time and hours spent?
- Clients name?
- Horses involved?
- Goals for the session?
- Equine Assisted Activities?
- Outcome?
- What happened during the event and if you noted anything special?
- Who were the facilitators?
- Who volunteered?

If an accident should occur, record the time, date, place, horses and people involved.

Tell what happened, as well as what treatment and follow up was given.

It is recommended that you have insurance to do this work.

On the next page are some sample forms we use for Healing Horses & Armed Forces. They are some of the forms you will receive at our Grand Prix Course.

The first form entitled, GROUP ACTIVITY NOTES has to do with the initial information about the participants. There are three things to note.

GROUP ACTIVITY NOTES

Name	Initial evaluation/remarks 1. According to the returned medical and risk form. 2. What we observed when participant arrived. (Emotional or physical) 3. Objectives, of the program.

ACTIVITY PROGRESS NOTE

Describe what you did. What arena, what horses, what obstacles? Attach the program schedule with descriptions to the notes with any outstanding occurrences.

Did all the group participate: yes, no

OUTCOME:

What happened? Horses reactions?   Did any significant events happen and to which participants? Pick out a few key participants outcome and an overall outcome of the group. In general, what did the group gain by participation?

*Use one worksheet for each activity.

ACTIVITY: (2)

Describe what we did. What arena, what horses, what obstacles? Attach the program schedule with descriptions to the notes.

Did all the group participate: yes, no

OUTCOME:

What happened? Horses reactions? Did any significant events happen and to which participants? Pick out a few key participant outcomes and an overall outcome of the group. In general, what did the group gain be participation?

Created by Michelle Weed

Near Miss or Safety Incident Report / Date _____ .

Victim Name _____ Male/Female _____ Age _____ Staff/Client _____

Activity _____ Area of the Facility _____

Weather Temp: _____ Rain _____ Wind _____ Snow _____ Visibility

---

1. Was this a Near Miss? (A near miss has the potential for serious injury, although no actual injury occurred.) Yes _____ No _____ **If Yes, Skip to section 4**

---

2. Type of Incident: Injury _____ Illness _____ Mot/Beh _____ Other _____
   (Examples of MOTIVATIONAL/BEHAVIORAL incidents include refusing to participate, running away, assaultive behavior, suicidal indication, or sexual or domestic violence.)

---

3. Did the victim leave the property?   NO _____ YES _____ If yes, Date? _____

   Complete A through C only if your answer to #3 is Yes.
   A. Was the victim evacuated?   NO _____ YES _____ If Yes, method?
   B. Did the victim visit a medical facility? NO _____ YES _____ If Yes, length of stay?
   C. Did the victim return to the event?   NO _____ YES _____ If Yes, on what date?

---

4. Complete the following sections as they apply:

TYPE OF INJURY OR ILLNESS (prioritize major applicable categories 1, 2, 3, etc.)

___Abrasion   ___Dental   ___Pre exist Ill/Injury?
___Anaphylaxis   ___Dislocation   ___Puncture
___Allergy   ___Exhaustion   ___Respiratory
___AMS (altitude)   ___Fever   ___Skin Problem
___Blister   ___Fracture   ___Sprain
___Burn   ___Frostbite   ___Strain
___Cardiac   ___Hypothermia   ___Suicide ideation
___Concussion   ___Infection   ___Tendonitis
___Contusion   ___Laceration   ___Urinary Tract

Other _____

PROGRAM ACTIVITY (prioritize major applicable categories 1, 2, 3, ETC.)

___Backpacking   ___Initiative   ___Service
___Camping   ___Kayaking   ___Skiing
___Carving   ___Rafting   ___Snowshoeing
___Climbing wall   ___Rappelling   ___Swimming
___Cooking   ___Rock climbing   ___Vehicle/Van
___Cycle   ___Ropes course   ___Urban activity
___Hiking   ___Running
___Horse   ___Sailing

Other _____

IMMEDIATE CAUSE (prioritize major applicable categories 1,2,3, etc.)

___Altitude   ___Fall/slip   ___Improper technique
___Alcohol   ___Falling rock   ___Medication
___Clothing   ___Fast water   ___Missing/lost
___Dehydration   ___Hazardous animal   ___Psychological
___Drugs   ___Hostile bystander   ___Misbehavior
___Exceeded ability   ___Improper equipment   ___Unfit
___Exhaustion   ___Improper instruction   ___Weather
___Fail to follow instruction   ___Improper supervision

Other

_____

_____

Put an X above where the client was ill or injured.

NARRATIVE:

Describe the incident completely. Include how the incident happened, any medical treatment given, and the finale outcome.

_____

_____

_____

ANALYSIS: Include any observations, recommendations, or suggestions regarding how the incident could have been prevented.

_____

_____

_____

_____

_____

Report prepared by: _____ Position: _____ Date: _____

Staff involved: _____

Comments by Personal Development Specialist: _____

_____

_____

_____

PDS Signature: _____ DATE: _____

Comments by Equine Specialist: _____

_____

_____

_____

ES Signature: _____ DATE: _____

Equine Incident Report   Date_____

Horse Name _____ Staff _____ Time _____

Type of incident _____ Was the horse removed from activity? _____

What horses or participants were involved? _____

Explain what happened? _____
_____
_____

Where did the injury occur? (Location on property) _____

What was administered? _____ Was the vet called? _____

Please put an X on the horse below in the area the horse was injured.

*Rising Moon Ranch 27501 Cumberland Road, Tehachapi, CA 93561 661 821-0482
*Twin Oaks Veterinary Services Chris & Lara.................661 867-2554 - 661 809-0597

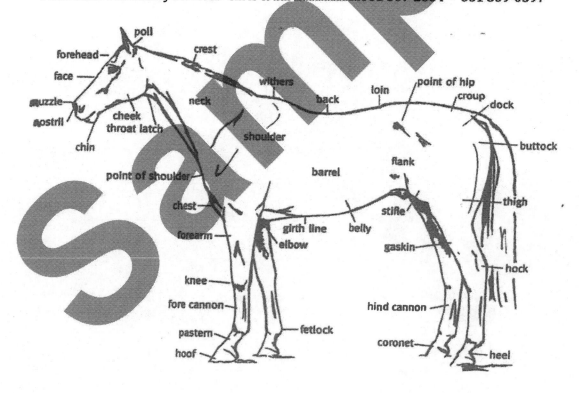

Created by Charisse Rudolph ©

Before a program, you will need to make a program schedule. The schedule is based on whether you will have individuals or groups. If you are meeting with client(s) once a week, following your initial consultation set a schedule with goals. Change the goals as needed.

Be prepared, clients will tell you their goal, but often times the goal changes. It is a good idea to plan the day's event with your team ahead of time.

On the morning of the event, go over the plan with all those involved before participants arrive. The schedule does not always go as planned, so it is important that all staff and volunteers clearly understand their roles for the event.

Below is a sample group program schedule. In addition, I have included an introduction program schedule that was printed out and given to some VIPs that came to the ranch.

SAMPLE PROGRAM:

2014 Holiday Horses & Christmas Cheer Program Agenda

ON THIS DAY WE HAD THREE VOLUNTEERS.
1. HORSE, & PROGRAM LOGISTICS INSTRUCTIONS WERE IN GREEN **(G)**
2. MUSIC PERSON INSTRUCTIONS WERE IN BLUE **(B)**
3. PAPER WORK INSTRUCTIONS WERE IN RED **(R)**

9:30 **(B)** Music on

9:40 PARTICIPANT ARRIVAL
(R) Greet participants, have them go to tack room and **sign all the paper work.**
(B) Lower music

10:00 CIRCLE UP in the indoor arena. Do introductions, tell them about the day, safety, challenge by choice, point out restrooms, etc. Do Group Challenge/Ice Breaker.
(Human Knot, Yurt circle, Have you ever? It will depend on participants.)

10:30 REGROUP, and ask participants to share what they hope to get out of the day? Pass around basket of rocks. Teach them the Heart-Focused Breathing and Quick Coherence techniques. Today we will practice Heart Focused Breathing before each equine assisted activity.
Ask participants to do a five-minute walk-about thinking about how they can add whatever attribute they have chosen and how it can be added to their present situation.)
Bathroom Break

(G) If weather is good this initiative will be done in the front half of the outside arena with Brie, Patch, and Lilly
11:00 - 11:15　　　　　**OBSERVE THE HERD**
HEART FOCUSED BREATHING

(G) Brie, Patch, Lilly
11:15 – 11:45　　　　　**INTUITION**
HEART-FOCUSED BREATHING

(G) ~FEED HORSES LUNCH IN THEIR STALLS~

11:45 – 12:15　　　　　**MOVING ENERGY**
HEART-FOCUSED BREATHING

(B) *PUT ON SERIOUS MUSIC COUNTRY during Lunch in barn*

12:30 -1245　　　　**LUNCH & PING PONG (Indoor Area)**

(G) Take chairs out of the indoor arena and put in two of the plastic jump holders and one pole going across, 2 feet high, have two poles on the ground either side of jump. Lets do this activity with Lily (horse). Then put chairs from indoor table in a circle around the Indian carpet in the yoga studio.

91

1:00 – 2:00   <u>**COME TOGETHER**</u>
HEART-FOCUSED BREATHING

2:00 - 2:30   DRUMMING DEMO in Yoga studio and quick demo on the HeartMath Techniques

(G) While we are doing a drumming demo, put mini horses and outdoor chairs into round ring. Have 6 small buckets ready to be labeled. Have cut up carrots, Safe Choice, cut up apples, some apple wafers, in each bucket. Fill buckets half way. Put out felt pens, 3x5 cards & tape.

2:10- 2:45   <u>**RED LIGHT, GREEN LIGHT**</u> (energy exercise)
HEART-FOCUSED BREATHING

(G) Afterwards, help participants and volunteers put a chair for themselves in the indoor arena by the big doors into a circle. We will pass out gifts and do final debrief after WWP and Path papers are all signed.

3:00 – 4:00   SIGN WWP EVALUATIONS, PATH ATTENDANCE SHEETS & DEBRIEF.

1. Sign Wounded Warriors Project Evaluations **(R)**
2. Sign Paths Attendance Sheets **(R)**
3. Come back to indoor arena.
4. Gather for final group debrief.
5. After participants leave staff and volunteer debrief.

NOTES:
Once again, I would like to mention at our programs, we teach and practice the HEART-FOCUSED BREATHING techniques and methods to relieve stress and think clearly. However, that doesn't mean you have to do this method for your participants.

Before a program commences, those who are working the program have gone over the schedule and discussed the equine activities we are going to do. You can also add a description for those who are not familiar with the activities.

I hope by now it goes without saying that this is Plan #A. Depending on what happens during the hours spent, you may have to change things up or allow an activity to be taken into a different direction. You have to go with the flow, be creative, spontaneous, and follow the needs of the participants and horses while working within the structure of the activity.

One time I had a participant tell me she had to go check on something, and she drove away and didn't come back until the end of the program. It was a family program. Thinking she would be back, we changed the activity and went in a different direction to meet the needs of the family she left.

VIP PROGRAM SCHEDULE

NOTE:

You will want to get people who are influential behind you. One way to do this is to invite them to see a program, or you can do a demonstration. Below is an example of a program explained to the VIPs who came to observe one of our programs. This schedule not only explained what they were watching, but it explained why Equine Assisted Activities are so powerful.

Introduction to Healing Horses & Armed Forces
at Rising Moon Ranch

Program Schedule

If you have been invited to observe on deck, here is what the Healing Horses & Armed Forces (HHAAF) program is doing and why. Because the participants are sharing personal and private confidences, a licensed therapist and an equine specialist are involved in every activity. Charisse Rudolph is the CEO/Founder of *Healing Horses & Armed Forces.* She is certified Level Two with the *Equine Assisted Growth and Learning Association* (EAGALA) and is an Equine Specialist in Mental Health and Learning. In addition, she is certified with the *Professional Association of Therapeutic Horsemanship International* (PATH Intl.) as an Equine Specialist in Mental Health. She has been in the field of personal development since 1992, bringing the horses into the work in 2001. Kelly Arbaut, ACSW, is a California-licensed therapist for trauma victims and is also certified with PATH Intl. She has been working with horses for over 20 years, and she is the CEO/Founder of the non-profit, *Kelly's Therapeutic Riders,* that helps children and adults with disabilities.

We would be pleased to have you stay for lunch, allowing us to talk to you afterwards. If you are unable to join us, we can talk by Skype or telephone. Please check your calendar so we can contact you to make a date for any questions you may have and to discuss strategies on support for our program.

(Your info.)

Thank you for taking the time to learn about Healing Horses & Armed Forces.

8:00 FACILITATOR ARRIVAL
Western Attire, T-shirts with logo.

9:00 PARTICIPANT ARRIVAL
Meet and greet. The volunteers will collect all paperwork and ensure everyone is accounted for. The volunteers will confirm that all risk and medical forms, etc. are signed. At this time, the volunteers for the day will notify the lead facilitator making he or she aware regarding specific red-flag health issues. The instructors will then direct participants into the arena and get started with the day's activities.

9:30: INTRODUCTION
In a circle, the instructors and then the participants will introduce themselves.

9:45: ICEBREAKER
Yurt Circle or stand ups.
Reason: This gets the participants engaged and laughing, releasing endorphins, and is the starting brick toward building trust and communication.

10:00: ROCKS & WALK ABOUT
Reason: Sometimes in life, we don't know what we want, but we know what we don't want. The rocks include a positive affirmation that can point them towards building a new and better tomorrow. It is a good starting point; it takes them to a deeper level. After they have taken five minutes to walk around and think about how they would like to add that affirmation to their life or relationship, we come back to the circle and share. Everything we do is "challenge by choice," including sharing personal thoughts. We give our participants a choice to share or not share.
(At this time, one of my staff tells me about any health issues that I need to know.)

10:30: INTUITION
Each participant will separately visit the horses, choosing and naming the one he or she would most want to form a relationship with and love. Regroup and share.
Reason: We all have a sixth sense and when we start to trust and listen to it, we become more compassionate, understanding, trusting, and confident. This exercise also allows the facilitators to see where the participants are emotionally, especially after the participants name their chosen horse.

Q: When do you see that characteristic in your partner?

Q: How does the name you chose represent the character you saw in the horse?

Snack and bathroom break

Outside Arena

11:10 - 11:45: LIFE & DEPLOYMENT

With three horses in the arena, divide participants into two groups. Give one group the task of getting three horses into a temporary corral that they build. Give a second group the task of getting three horses and putting one horse into each corner of the three sides of the arena (no halters, or ropes).

Reason: Here we get to see the dynamics of the relationships and how each person responds to one another. This is the meat and potatoes of the program. It tells us where we need to go next. In a full day, program or multiple days we would keep working with the couples to smooth out the bumps and give them tools to cope better with their relationship. In addition to the equine assisted activities, the participants learn new methods to control and calm their anger. Horses learn a conditioned response when they are learning new things about life, just as humans do.

12:00 - 12:45: NEW BEGINNINGS

In any relationship, there is yourself, your mate, and your relationship. All three have to be loved and cared for or they will wilt and die. In the arena, the path before the participants represents their relationships with their spouses/partners. Participants will think about what obstacles may get in their way of experiencing the relationship they would like to have. Using the props that we have put in the arena, the participants will choose objects that represent some of the possible obstacles they have considered and place those objects inside the path. Next, the participants choose some of the attributes that will help them overcome the obstacles this day and in their future lives.

Reason: At this juncture, not only the therapist and equine specialist, but also the spouse or partner, will likely hear things that may have never been said before. Fears and challenges can be readily dealt with once they are apparent. The chosen attributes are added to whatever the rock represented at the beginning of the day, thereby permitting the participants to continue building positive coping skills throughout the program. The horse adds to the dynamics because the horse senses and reacts to what the participants are saying and/or the energy they are giving off. When the participants are able to get the horse to respond and cooperate, they learn to use the same communication methods in their personal lives. Participants are asked throughout the day their horse's name and what the horse represents for them.

1:00: Debriefing

A short debriefing is held within a circle of chairs, indoors, and with calming background music. The concept of a "Council" and "The Recipe for Writing a Love Letter" or "The Seven Levels Deep" is provided in written form and is discussed. In ending the program, participants are then granted a Certificate of Completion.

Reason: "Council" is a tool that is Native American by nature and helpful in conflict resolution. Charisse Rudolph has been using and teaching this communication method for many years. "The Recipe for the Love Letter" is another tool used to find out how participants are feeling about a situation, but it is not meant to be shared. Ending the program with "The Seven Levels Deep" gives participants new, additional tools to take home for working out conflicts. What makes the challenge greater for a military couple is the couple must also deal with the effects of PTS or TBI.

1:30: Post-Workshop Lunch

---

* Depending on your unique talents and inspirations you can create a program for your clients with your own special style. This is part of my style and a typical half-day program in 2012. In 2014, I added the HeartMath techniques to all of my events and drumming. In fact, "Red Light, Green Light," is an energy activity that I created with horses and drumming.

When we do two or more day retreats, yoga can be added as well as therapeutic art. We also can teach some of the more advanced HeartMath techniques. In addition, we have planned a community kitchen for therapeutic cooking.

I have included, a sheet that gives you more information on how to do HeartMath's, Quick Coherence® technique which includes Heart-Focused Breathing™. In addition, I have added a list of possible props, and attributes that we use at our equine assisted programs. You can laminate the words. Our laminated words are two-three inches wide.

HeartMath's Quick Coherence® Technique

Step 1- Heart Focus

Focus your attention on the area around your heart.

Step 2- Heart-Focused Breathing

Maintain your heart focus and, while breathing, imagine that your breath is flowing in and out through the heart area. Breathe casually, just a little deeper than normal. *Suggestion: Inhale 5 seconds; exhale 5 seconds (or whatever rhythm is comfortable).*

Step 3- Heart Feeling

Make a sincere attempt to experience a regenerative feeling such as appreciation or care for someone or something in your life. Suggestion: Try to re-experience the feeling you have for someone you love, a pet, a special place, an accomplishment, etc., or focus on a feeling of calm or ease. You could also breathe in feelings of courage, dignity, honor or integrity.

PROPS CAN INCLUDE

Swim Noodles
Buckets
Pails
Small and Medium Hula-Hoops
Plastic Shovels
Stuffed Animals
Butterfly Nets

Plastic Army Men
Halloween Toys
Play Ball and Chain
Play Handcuffs
Barbie Dolls
Play Money
Squirt Guns
Hats

Cones
Mardi Gras Necklaces
Patriotic Items
Plastic Chains
Balls
Rubber Snakes

**I went to the 99-cent store and had a great time picking out different items.
Get Creative!**

Sixty Positive Attributes

Kind
Intelligent
Hardworking
Loyal
Attractive
Down-to-Earth
Goofy
Creative
Accepting
Strong
Friendly
Flexible
Nurturing
Thoughtful
Confident
Optimistic
Respectful
Determined
Skilled
Helpful

Motivated
Insightful
Funny
Patient
Realistic
Honest
Generous
Modest
Serious
Independent
Trusting
Resilient
Cheerful
Self-Directed
Reliable
Relaxed
Listener
Brave
Courageous
Decisive

Enthusiastic
Forgiving
Humble
Sensitive
Organized
Selfless
Practical
Mature
Focused
Courteous
Grateful
Open-Minded
Positive
Responsible
Cooperative
Frugal
Tolerant
Innovative
Balanced
Sobriety

Choose the attributes you like and have them laminated.

Making Money, Being of Service with your Horses and Getting Started

When the field of equine assisted services began, I thought I was creating something new. I had been doing team-building and challenge course work since 1992. We did large programs for one to several days in length, coaching and facilitating corporations and private schools. In addition, I had been riding horses since I was two years old, and I knew them in and out. In 2000, I was looking at all the team-building activities we had done throughout the years and started thinking of how we could recreate them with the horses being involved. I knew how horses had affected my life, and I wanted to share that gift with others. Then I heard about EAGALA and joined them in 2001.

EAGALA members in those days mainly did one-on-one type programs (One client, one equine specialist, and one mental health specialist.) Greg Kersten, who is now the CEO of the O.K. Corral, www.okcorralseries.com one of the original founders of EAGALA did great work with boys who were incarcerated and youth ranches. Kids who were displaced because of some type of personal or family trouble were some of the early recipients of EAP, as well as people dealing with eating disorders, addictions, and other communities who needed the added magic that our equine partners could share.

The field of Equine Assisted Activities is now wide open, and whatever population is your calling you can work with, as long as that community has an urgent need. Find your niche and bring your own uniqueness into your programs or events. If you want to make money, which we all need to do in order to feed our horses and pay our bills, do group programs and *Retreats*! Do *Joint Ventures* and *Retreats*. *Retreats* can be a full day to several days in length. Let your imagination run wild.

Rising Moon Ranch offers three *"Train the Trainer,"* programs. In our Grand Prix Course we share information on how to do a *retreat*, what to look for in doing a *joint venture*, and we will share all of our forms, from the "Let's Get Started" form, all the way through the "Thank You for Participating," form.

Every form you could possibly need for your clients, volunteers, staff, and more. Path Intl. looked at all our forms in order for us to become a Premiere Accredited Center. Our forms are very thorough! (Check with your attorney to make sure they are right for your programs.) In addition, you will receive coaching calls to answer questions and help you problem solve; we will help you design your own program, guide you in marketing, and help you write a business plan of your own. On the next pages you can read all about what we offer.

"The Soul is dyed the color of its thoughts.
Day by day, what you do is who you become. Your integrity is your destiny – it is the light that guides your way."

Heraclitus

Charisse Rudolph is fiercely committed to guiding Equine Assisted Coaches to achieve their dreams of equine partnership to the fullest possibility. Having Equine Assisted Services recognized and valued can sometimes be a challenge. She knows what it is like to offer such a magnificent modality for personal growth and healing, and put everything into achieving that goal.

Anyone involved with horses, and personal development of any kind knows how much value EAS offers people who are on their life journey. A natural human-equine connection has been going on since the beginning of time. If you are looking for a proven professional who can guide you through the ins and outs of being successful in this business, who knows horses like the back of her hand, who has massive experience in the field of Equine Assisted Coaching and can help you design your own unique program, you've come to the right place.

With 23 years of experience working with teams of amazing clients and guiding them to achieve remarkable success, my mission and commitment is to enable you to offer the best equine assisted services any where around. In addition, I invite all coaches to do a *Joint Venture/Retreat* at my Rising Moon Ranch or at your own facility.

It would be my pleasure to guide you to achieve the results you desire, or the life you imagine in the Rising Moon Ranch *Train the Trainer*. You have your choice of the Six-Month Grand Prix Course, our Three-Month, Sage Coaching Services, or our One-Day Boot Camp for Equine Assisted Coaching.

We all need a coach or trainer at some time, whether it is for our horses or ourselves. If you are ready to turn yesterday's dreams into the reality of today, fill out the Grand Prix application and send it to us, or call for your free consultation.

What you get at the Grand Prix Course

	VALUE
One-day Boot-Camp for Equine Assisted Coaches.	$325.00
2-Day Live Event in Creating your Program	$1,800
Grand Prix Online Audio	$47.00
A book, The Art of Facilitation, with 28 Equine Assisted Activities	$25.00
Grand Prix Membership with Private Facebook Group	
Strategies and Handout for Marketing	$147.00
Strategies and Handout on How to do a Retreat	$147.00
Strategies and Handout on How to do a Joint Venture	$147.00
Strategies and Handout on How to do a Clinic	$147.00
One-on-One Support with Designing your Own Unique Program	$297.00
One-on-One Support in Finding your Community to be of Service	$297.00
One-on-One Guidance with your Strategic Business Plan	$297.00
Equine Assisted Coaching - Forms for Clients, Staff, Horses and Volunteers	$4,000.00
Facilitation Teleseminar	$197.00
Equine Assisted Coaching Teleseminar	$197.00
Strategic Business Plan Teleseminar	$197.00
Marketing Teleseminar	$197.00
Certificate	
Refreshments, and Lunches @ Rising Moon Ranch at Joint Venture.	$72.00
Opportunity to do a Joint Venture at Rising Moon Ranch with Charisse	Priceless
Total Value (After 2016, call for tuition special)	$8,338
Special 2015 -2016 Tuition	$4,997

For every person you bring through 2016, you will receive a $1000.00 discount on the "Grand Prix Course," $100.00 off on "Sage Coaching," and $50.00 off on the "One-Day, Boot Camp for Equine Assisted Coaching." Ask about our group discounts.

Application for the Grand Prix Course at Rising Moon Ranch

We are committed to giving you all we can give. Being of service is our honor. We know we have a lot to share, but we need to make sure we are a good fit and that this is something that will be of benefit. We are willing to mentor you and share all that we have if you are passionate about your direction.

We feel the more we help others to lead, the more people we can be of service to through you.

We look forward to getting to know you better as we read your answers below:

_____

1. Full name _____ Best email address _____

2. Please describe how you can use the Grand Prix Course to enrich your life?

_____

_____

_____

3. How will it benefit the community you wish to serve?

_____

_____

4. Dream, Imagine, Believe, and have Faith are words that hang on the office wall. With these four words in mind, please describe what your future in Equine Assisted Coaching could look like if you were able to do what you want.

_____

_____

_____

5. How will your success benefit you and your chosen community?

_____

_____

6.   On a scale from 1 – 10, how committed to your vision are you? (1-low, 10-high)

7.   What gifts/resources do you have that will help you fulfill this vision?

_____

_____

_____

8.   What obstacles could stop you from fulfilling your vision?

   a. What limiting beliefs could get in your way?
_____

   b. What emotions could get in your way?
_____

   c. What people/circumstances could get in your way?
_____

   d. What is bigger: your commitment to your success or the obstacles that could get in your
      way?
_____

9.   If you were to become a member of the Grand Prix Course, what is it that we
     offer that most attracts you?

   ()   The knowledge you will gain in facilitating? Facilitating people to
        advance in their lives with horses involved is different than regular
        coaching because the horses reflect the energy we are sending out.

   ()   Becoming an expert in the field of Equine Assisted Coaching? Whether
        you are a full time coach or just getting into the field of equine assisted
        coaching, the more you learn the more you will be looked at as the
        expert. First you have to make it, then you have to master it, and then
        you will matter!

   ()   The joyous life you will have being able to work with your horses?
        Instead of having to make time to see or ride your horses, now you will
        have to make time to do other things.

   ()   The life style: Working for yourself, being outdoors, creating your own
        schedule is the best feeling in the world.

()   Having someone mentoring you with all the experience, knowledge and know how that you need in order to be successful?

Other _____

10.   What would you need to get out of the Grand Prix Course to make it worthwhile to you?

_____

_____

_____

11.   What do you imagine will change for you out of making this investment in yourself?

_____

_____

_____

12.   Why would you join the Grand Prix Course?

_____

_____

_____

Please accept my application to become a Member of the Grand Prix Course.

_____   _____

Signature   Date

Thank you for completing your application to become a Member of the Grand Prix Course. The reason for us sharing everything is to help you succeed. In addition, we use the tuition to support our non-profit Healing Horses & Armed Forces.

We feel honored that you are taking this big leap to invest in yourself. We are excited to support you to take your life as an equine assisted coach to a completely new level.

Sage Coaching Services @ Rising Moon Ranch

Charisse Rudolph and Rising Moon Ranch are fiercely committed to guiding Equine Assisted Coaches to fulfilling their dreams of equine partnership. Weekly coaching calls keep you on track and accountable, moving forward toward your goals. In addition, we offer informational materials, trainings, joint ventures and retreats.

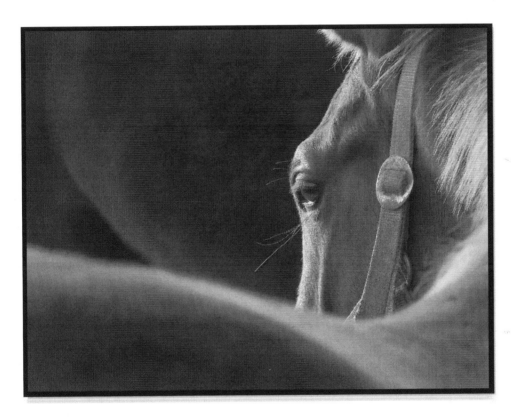

A Transformative Coaching System That Brings Results.

A person with many years of experience is called a Sage. They pass on wisdom to others who are seeking. Equine Assisted Services can add value to your customers, but it can be a challenge for your clients to recognize the benefits. Often, an Equine Assisted Coach (EAC) has to work two jobs just to make ends meet. At Sage Coaching Services, we show the EAC how to put all the pieces together through weekly action plans, strategizing and problem solving.

SAGE Coaching Services Promises To:

1. **S**HARE our lifetime of experience, and give you advice and direction on how to succeed.
This is our Mission!

2. **A**SSIST you in achieving the results you want with a weekly action plan.
This is our Commitment!

3. **G**UIDE you to be at the top in your field by helping you find your niche, build your program, and solve the challenges along the way.
This is our Passion!

4. **E**MPOWER you to be the best Equine Assisted Coach you can be for the transformation of your clients.
This is our Honor!

STEP 1 – SHARE to succeed.

Our mission is to share our knowledge and years of experience to those who are newer to Equine Assisted Coaching (EAC) or to those who want more detail about how to succeed. We started out in an age when experiential coaching was in its infancy. We have seen and been through changes and challenges in our field. Through the years we have been successful, but we have made our share of mistakes to possess the experiential knowledge and insight that we can share today.

A. With Step 1 you will begin to understand how to go from the first meeting with your prospective client to the end result.

B. You will receive all our forms on a thumb drive. Forms that you can re-create for your own organization and use.

C. In addition, we will take you through one of our programs and detail the reasoning behind each step or part of the plan.

D. We will assist you in creating your own program and discuss the reasons behind the strategic plan for your event.

STEP 2 – ASSIST in a weekly action plan for results.

Not only will we share with you an in-depth understanding of Equine- Assisted- Activities, but we will also give you a weekly one-on-one, 45-minute, coaching call that will keep you moving toward your goal.

A. In Step 2, we will help you to find your niche market, which is the community you are most passionate about serving.

B. We will take a closer look at your unique gifts and how you would like to share that within your niche market.

C. Then, we will assist you in creating a program, joint venture, or retreat for the community you have chosen.

D. In addition, we will discuss different methods to get more clients.

STEP 3 – GUIDE to build and problem solve.

Building and problem-solving is the name of the game. There is a lot to think about (i.e. clients, horses, volunteers, staff, insurance, business plans, paper work, web page, program outlines).

A. In Step 3, we will guide you in designing a Demonstration Day for the community you are passionate about serving. We will help you decide the hours, the day, the time of year, what Equine-Assisted-Activities to use, what paper work you will want to create for the day, etc.

B. We will discuss ideas to bring awareness to your Equine-Assisted Business.

C. We will go over what forms to use and when to use them.

D. We will really make sure you understand how to facilitate between the horses and your customers.

E. We will look at the dynamics of your herd. Horses have different characters just like people. Some are introverts and some are extroverts. We can help you combined different horses for different activities and clients.

STEP 4 – EMPOWERING YOU to transform and enroll clients.

Part of the process of success is gaining confidence in yourself. This helps clients so they trust your judgment and enroll in your services.

A. You can only support the transformation of your clients to the degree of your own transformation. We will show you our #1 secret about getting coherent, so you are feeling whole and have your mind, heart and nervous system working as one. It will change your life and help your clients to succeed.

B. We will help you enroll your clients by giving you some simple strategies that will enhance your ability to be heard.

C. We will share some techniques that will help you define who you are and where you want to go in the field of helping humans with horses.

To Sum it up, Rising Moon Ranch offers three different *"Train the Trainer,"* programs (which include the book, "The Art of Facilitation, with 28 Equine Assisted Activities.")

1) The Grand Prix, Deluxe, no hold back, 6-month intensive.

2) Sage Coaching Services, 3-month, one-on-one, weekly coaching call.

3) A One-Day Boot Camp for Equine Assisted Coaching

"Train the Trainers," at Rising Moon Ranch helps you discover:

1. The five secrets you need to know in order to enroll clients.

2. The contracts and forms you need to limit liable.

3. What you should know about doing a joint venture.

4. If you have to be incorporated and what insurance you need.

5. How to use your unique talents to design a niche in which you are the expert.

6. Why retreats are so much more profitable and how to put one together.

7. How to think clearly even when you are out of your comfort zone.

8. How to choose the correct horses for the equine assisted activity.

9. How to create a series of equine assisted activities for your specific client community.

10. How to make a strategic business plan.

11. How to create your mission statement and why it matters.

Train the Trainer One-Day Boot Camp

Charisse Rudolph
27501 Cumberland Rd.
Tehachapi, CA.
93561

EAGALA Certified 2001& 2011
PATH Certified 2014

One-day Event "Boot Camp"
Equine Assisted Coaching

COME JOIN US
At the Training for Equine Assisted Coaching, you'll discover new activities, how to add your uniqueness into your programs, how to get stared, and we will discuss the philosophy of facilitation.

Along with the training you will receive a book I am just perfecting for coaches called, The Art of Facilitation, with 28 Equine Assisted Activities.

We look forward to meeting you
Limited openings for training.

Rising Moon Ranch
Premiere Accredited Site with PATH Intl.

Rising Moon Ranch
www.risingmoonranch.org

Details for the Upcoming Training:

When: August 1st, 2015
Where: Rising Moon Ranch
Time : 9:00 – 4:00
27501 Cumberland Rd.
Tehachapi, CA. 93561
424-835-0482

Training $325. Checks received by July 4th
Early Bird Special $249. If checks received before July 4th.
Snacks and beverages only will be provided.
Arrive early to sign paper work.

(Please note, prices are subject to change, please call for updates.)

110

If you are on the fence about taking the *"Grand Prix Course," "Sage Coaching Services,"* or the *"One-Day Boot Camp for Equine Assisted Coaches,"* please call Rising Moon Ranch for a "free thirty-minute consultation and to check our current pricing."
424-835-0482

6 - Month Intensive ~Grand Prix Coaching Course~

3 – Month, Weekly ~Sage Coaching Services~

1 - Day, Boot Camp ~Equine Assisted Coaching~

Book – The Art of Facilitation, with 28 Equine Assisted Activities

~Retreats, Joint Ventures, Trainings at your Location Available upon Request ~

CALL FOR DATES & INFORMATION

In addition, did you know you can receive at least 10 hours of credit with EAGALA for continuing education if you are already certified and you are up for renewal?

If you need an expert to help you accelerate in the field of Equine Assisted Services, or experiential based coaching, give us a call for a free thirty-minute consultation.

Charisse Rudolph, Rising Moon Ranch,
risingmoonranch@gmail.com
Trainings; www.risingmoonranch.net
Programs; www.risingmoonranch.org
27501 Cumberland Rd.
Tehachapi, CA. 93561
424-835-0482

(For each person you bring through 2016, you will receive $1,000 off tuition for the Grand Prix Course, $100. off Sage Coaching and $50.00 off the One-day Boot Camp)

FOOTNOTES

(1) Edgar H. Schein, "The Mechanism of Change," in W.G. Bennis, K.D. Benne, R. Chin, eds. "The Planning of Change" (New York: Holt, Reinhart & Winston, 1969) Pg. 99

(2) Norman Cousins, Human Options: "An Autobiographical Notebook."
New York: W.W. Norton and Company. Pg. 16
Cousins, Norman. *The Human Options: An Autobiographical Notebook*. New York: Norton, 1981. 16. Print.

(3) Walsh and G. Golins, "The Exploration of the Outward Bound Process."
Denver: Colorado Outward Bound School. 1975 pg. 2

(4) Rhodes, "The Problem of individual Change" pg.2

(5) Charles E. Silberman, "Crisis in the Classroom: The Remaking of American Education." New York: Vantage Books. 1971, pg. 379-380

(6) Lee Snooks, et. Al. Bacstop, Battle Creek, Michigan: Michigan Department of Education Title IV-C. Battle Creek Public Schools, n.d.pg. 77

(7) Ann Beck, "Hawaii Bound: Operations Manual," Honolulu, Hawaii: Hawaii Bound School, Inc., 1979, pg. 27

(8) Gerald Weinstein, et. Al. "Education of Self: A Trainer's Manual,"
Amherst, Massachusetts: Mandala. 1976, pg. 161-165

(9) Ibid., pg. 127

THE END ☺

Made in the USA
San Bernardino, CA
15 November 2016